Regenerative Agri BLUEPRINT for Small Farms

Enrich Soil Fertility, Boost Vegetable Yield, and Optimize Profits to Become Wealthy

Sherri Todd

Copyright ©2024 by Sherri Todd

All rights reserved. No part of this publication may be reproduced, stored or transmitted in any form or by any means electronic, mechanical, photocopying, recording, scanning or otherwise without written permission from the publisher. It is illegal to copy this book, post it to a Website, or distribute it by any other means without permission.

Sherri Todd asserts the moral rights to be identified as the author of this work.

Sherri Todd has no responsibility for the persistence or accuracy of URLs for external third party internet Websites referred to in this publication and does not guarantee that any content on such websites is, or will remain accurate or appropriate.

Designations used by companies to distinguish their products are often claimed as trademarks. All brand names used in this book and on its cover are trademark names, service marks, trademarks, and registered trademarks of their respective owners. The publisher and the book are not associated with any product or vendor mentioned in this book. None of the companies referenced within the book have endorsed the book.

Violators of the copyright will face the full extent of the law.

First Edition

Dedication

Thanks to all the genie writers, farmers and gardeners. I dedicate this book to all those small farms that produce 70% of the food production, who care about the earth, and who work tirelessly toward making the world and the soil a better place.

About the Author

Meet Sherri Todd, a passionate gardener, nature enthusiast, and author dedicated to cultivating green spaces and nurturing the beauty of the natural world. With a lifelong love affair with plants and a deep-rooted appreciation for the wonders of the outdoors, she has spent years honing their skills and expertise in gardening.

From humble beginnings tending to a small backyard plot to transforming sprawling landscapes into thriving havens of biodiversity, she believes in the transformative power of gardening to enrich lives and connect individuals with the earth.

Sherri seeks to inspire and empower others to embrace the joys of gardening, whether they're seasoned green thumbs or budding enthusiasts. Focusing on sustainable practices, organic gardening techniques, and the timeless wisdom passed down through generations, she shares invaluable insights, practical tips, and heartfelt anecdotes to guide readers' gardening journeys.

Sherri's other passions, which she writes about, are Stocks, Business Entrepreneurship, Crystal Healing, Health & fitness, fly-fishing, Cooking, and more.

Table of Contents

Contents

Dedication 4

About the Author 6

Table of Contents 7

Introduction 17
    Key Principles of Regenerative Agriculture: 18
    Practices of Regenerative Agriculture: 19
    Importance of Soil Fertility: Nourishing theRoots of Crop Growth 20

        The Key to Crop Growth 21

        Meeting Crop Nutrient Requirements 21

        Nurturing Plantation Growth 22
    Goals of Boosting Vegetable Yield and Optimizing Profits: Cultivating Success inYour Farm or Garden 23

Chapter One — From theEarthy Depths to Fertile 27
Soil Health Assessment 30

        Factors in Soil Performance and Function 30

        Crop, Yield, Water Quality, and Weather Conditions 32
    Principles of Soil Health Assessment 33

        Fundamental Principle of Soil Health Assessment 33

        Understanding the Role of Soil Structure andComposition 33

        The Importance of Soil Biology and Microorganisms 34

        Emphasis on Soil Nutrient Balance 34

        Integrating Soil Conservation and Management 35
    Testing Soil Health in the Field 36

        Soil Texture Test 36

        Soil Structure Assessment 37

Soil pH Test 37

Nutrient Content Analysis 37

Biological Activity Test 38

Interpreting Test Results 38

The 4'R's of Soil Assessment 39

Right Source 39

Right Rate 40

Right Time 40

Right Place 40

Impact on Soil Management Decisions 41

Building Sustainable Topsoil 41

Composting 41

Cover Cropping 42

Crop Rotation 42

Case Studies of Successful Topsoil Improvement 43

Identifying Different Soil Types 44

Soil Texture 44

Soil Color 45

Composition and Structure 45

Impact on Water Retention, Nutrient Availability, andPlant Growth 46

Nutrient Analysis 47

Methodologies for Determining Soil Nutrient Content 47

Relevance of Nutrient Analysis in Soil Management 48

Techniques for Identifying Soil Types 49

Soil Spectroscopy 50

Remote Sensing 50

Soil Texture by Feel Method 51

Jar Test for Soil Composition 52

Basic pH Testing 52

Observing Plant Indicators and Weeds 53

Choosing the Right Technique 53

Chapter Two — Building SoilHealth (Part I) 55
Overview of Soil Fertility 55
Importance of Sustainable Practices inAgriculture 56
Cover Cropping Strategies 58

Definition and Purpose of Cover Cropping 58

Historical Implementation of Cover Cropping 58

Various Methods of Cover Cropping 59

Benefits of Cover Cropping 60

Selection of Cover Crops 62
Composting Techniques 66

Overview of Composting 66

Types of Composting Techniques 66

DIY Composting: Seven Steps 67

Preparing Quality Compost 69

Troubleshooting Common Composting Issues 71
Natural Fertilizer Application 71

Understanding Natural Fertilizers 71

Best Natural Fertilizers 72

Application Methods 73

Case Studies and Examples 74

Chapter Three — BuildingSoil Fertility (Part II) 75
Crop Rotation 75

What is Crop Rotation? 75

Advantages of Crop Rotation 76

Disadvantages of Crop Rotation 79

Management Requirements in Crop Rotation 80
Diversified Planting 83

Understanding Structural Diversity in Crop Systems 83

Strategies to Increase Crop Diversity 84

Implementing These Strategies 85

Popular Farm Diversification Strategies 85

Approachable Strategies for SustainableFarming 88

Conversion to Organic Farming 89

Low-Till and No-Till Farming Practices 89

Utilization of Renewable Energy Sources 90

Community Supported Agriculture (CSA) Programs 90

Companion Planting for Maximum Yield 91

What is Companion Planting? 91

Understanding the Companion Planting Chart 92

Effective Companion Planting Pairs 92

Avoiding Incompatible Pairings 93

Implementing Companion Planting in Your Garden 93

Real-World Examples of Companion Planting 94

Chapter Four — WaterManagement 98

Efficient Irrigation Practices 100

Best Irrigation Techniques 100

Surface Irrigation 100

Drip Irrigation 101

Sprinkler Irrigation 101

Subsurface Irrigation 102

Evaluating Irrigation Efficiency 102

Water-Use Efficiency Metrics 102

Factors Influencing Efficiency 103

Case Studies of Efficiency Rates 103

Enhancing Irrigation Efficiency for Farmers 104

Strategies for Increasing Efficiency 104

    Challenges and Solutions 106
    Smart Irrigation Practices 108

        Definition and Relevance 108

        Technological Innovations in Irrigation.................................... 108

        Case Studies: Implementation and Results............................... 110
    Watering Systems in Agriculture... 111

        Types of Watering Systems 111

        Selection Criteria for Watering Systems................................... 113
    Role of Water in Crop Health 115

        Water as a Critical Resource 115

        Effects of Water Quality and Quantity on Crops 116

        Case Studies: Impact of Water Management on CropHealth...... 117
    Rainwater Harvesting 119

        Introduction to Rainwater Harvesting 119

        Methods of Rainwater Harvesting.. 120

        Disadvantages and Limitations... 120

        Global Examples of Rainwater Harvesting 121

        Sustainability Assessment.. 122
    Soil Moisture Monitoring.. 123

        Techniques for Measuring Soil Moisture................................. 123

        Importance of Soil Moisture Monitoring.................................. 124

        Innovations in Soil Moisture Detection 125

        Devices and Tools for Soil Moisture Monitoring 126
    Conclusion... 127

Chapter Five — 130
    No-Till Farming 132

        Comparison with Traditional Till Farming............................... 132

        Benefits of No-Till for Soil Health 133
    Transformative Effects on Farms.. 133

        Soil Structure and Fertility Improvements............................... 133

Water Conservation and Erosion Control 134
Practical Methods for Implementing No-Till 135
Transition Strategies from Traditional Tillage 135
Equipment and Technology Used in No-Till Farming 135
Managing Crop Residues and Soil Cover 136
Agroforestry Integration 137
Agroforestry's Impact on Ecosystems and Crops 138
Agroforestry for Sustainability: 138
Benefits to Trees and Crop Fields: 139
Pest Management through Natural Means 140
Contrast with Synthetic Pest Management Methods: 141
Natural Biological Methods for Pest Control: 141
The Role of Natural Insecticides: 142
Addressing Severe Pest Infestations Naturally: 143
Conclusion 144
Future Directions and Emerging Trends inRegenerative Practices
.... 145

Chapter Six — Profit Optimization Techniques 147
Profitable Farming Practices: Evaluating theProfit Margins of
Different Farming Methods 148
Case Studies: Examples of Successful ProfitableFarming 148
Maximizing Efficiency inAgriculture 149
Techniques for Increasing Crop Yield 149
Reducing Wastage and Resource Management 149
Cost vs. Benefit Analysis 150
Consumer Demand for Organic Produce 150
Comparative Analysis of Farming Methods 151
Traditional vs. Modern Techniques 151
Impact on Long-Term Profitability 151
Marketing and Sales Tactics for AgriculturalProducts 152

Identifying Your Market 152

Branding and Positioning in Agriculture 153

Eight Key Marketing Strategies for Farmers 153

Planting the Most Profitable Produce 158

Selecting Crops for Maximum Profit 161
Diversifying Income Streams in Agriculture 163

Balancing Investment and Returns 163

Value-Added Products and Services 164

Agricultural Tourism and Educational Programs 164

Exploring Land Rental and Other Ventures 165

Exploring Sustainable Agricultural Models 166
The Pillars of Sustainability in Agriculture 169

The Four Cs: Conservation, Community, Culture andCommerce
.... 169

The Five Cs: Climate, Customers, Crops, Conservationand
Community 170
Implementing Sustainable Practices 172

Case Studies of Successful Sustainable Farms 173

Chapter Seven — Monitoringand Evaluation 177
Understanding Agricultural Health 177

Measuring, Monitoring, and Analyzing: Keys toProductivity 178

The Importance of a Proactive Approach 179
The Five Principles of Soil Health 180

Minimize Disturbance 181

Maximize Soil Cover 181

Diversify Plant Species 182

Maintain Living Roots Year-Round 183

Integrate Livestock 183
Yield Monitoring: The Link Between SoilHealth and Crop Output
.... 184

Definition and Purpose 184
Critical Factors for Yield Determination 185
Approaches to Yield Monitoring 186
Mapping Techniques 188
Financial Tracking and Analysis in Agriculture........................... 190
Purpose and Benefits.. 191
Methods of Agricultural Financial Analysis................................ 192
Common Financial Challenges in Agriculture 194

Chapter Eight — Modern Agricultural Challenges and 198
The Role of Real-Time Case Studies... 199
Challenge One — Water Scarcity and Irrigation Issues................ 200

Case Study: Implementation of Smart Irrigation Systems in Israel
....201
Challenge Two — Soil Degradation and Sustainability 203

Overview of Soil Health Issues and Sustainability Concerns...... 203

Case Study: Regenerative Agriculture Practices in Brazil........... 204
Challenge Three — Impact of Climate Change on Crop Production
....206

How Changing Climates Affect Agriculture 207

Case Study: Drought-Resistant Crops in Australia..................... 207
Successful Implementation Stories.. 209

Case Study One — Advanced Greenhouse Techniques in the
Netherlands 209

Case Study Two — Precision Farming Technologies in the USA 212
Lessons Learned from Other Small Farms: Historical Perspectives
....215

Mixed Farming Techniques in Small European Farms.............. 215
Cropping System Research.. 217

Integrated Pest Management (IPM) Systems 218

Case Study on Successful IPM Implementation in Kenya 218

Chapter Nine — Tools and Resources 221

Factors Influencing Crop Success 222
Essential Resources and Tools 223
   Recommended Reading and Literature 224
   Essential Tools and Equipment... 226
Farming Practices and Techniques 229
   Soil Preparation and Management.. 229
   Crop Selection and Rotation... 230
   Planting and Sowing... 231
   Nutrient Management and Fertilization..................................... 232
   Pest and Disease Control 233
   Harvesting and Post-Harvest Handling 234
Agricultural Technology and Software 235
   Useful Apps and Software for Farmers 236
   Emerging Technologies in Agriculture 238
Networking and Community Engagement inAgriculture 242
   The Role of Agricultural Networks 242
   Farmer-to-Farmer Networks and Knowledge Sharing 243
   Community Engagement and Local Support Systems 244
   The Impact of Social Media and Online Communities 245
Conclusion and Future Prospects... 247
   Challenges and Opportunities in SustainableAgriculture 248
   Future Trends and Developments 250

Chapter Ten — A SubstantialPath Forward 254
   Practical Strategies and Tips for Implementing Regenerative
   Agriculture 256

Page Left Blank Intentionally

Introduction

If you've picked up this book, I expect you to know about regenerative agriculture? If you don't, that's not an issue. I aim to teach, train and guide all green thumbs with the fundamentals of this art. So, what is regenerative agriculture? As fancy as it may sound, regenerative agriculture is not merely a farming technique; it's a holistic philosophy that fosters harmony between humans and nature. It revolves around nurturing ecosystems, promoting biodiversity, and restoring soil health. By embracing regenerative practices, we not only produce nutritious food but also contribute to mitigating environmental challenges such as water scarcity, deforestation, and land degradation.

Unlike conventional farming practices that often degrade soil health and rely heavily on external inputs, regenerative agriculture seeks to work with nature to create productive and maintainable landscapes. Let's delve into the core principles and practices that define regenerative agriculture and its significance in enriching soil fertility, boosting vegetable yield, and optimizing profits for your farm or garden.

Key Principles of Regenerative Agriculture:

At its core, regenerative agriculture is guided by several key principles that form the foundation of sustainable farming practices. These principles include:

Soil Health: Central to regenerative agriculture is the emphasis on soil health. Healthy soils are teeming with life, rich in organic matter, and possess good structure and fertility. Practices such as reduced tillage, cover cropping, crop rotations, and the use of organic amendments help improve soil health by enhancing biological activity, nutrient cycling, and water retention. Soil degradation poses a severe threat to agricultural productivity and ecosystem stability. By fostering soil health, farmers can safeguard their land against erosion, nutrient depletion, and desertification.

Biodiversity: Biodiversity is essential for ecosystem resilience and stability. Regenerative agriculture encourages the integration of diverse crops, cover crops, and agroforestry systems to support a wide range of beneficial organisms, including pollinators, predators, and soil microbes. The rampant clearing of forests for agricultural purposes has led to the loss of invaluable biodiversity and ecosystem services. Regenerative agriculture offers a better alternative by promoting agroforestry, which integrates trees into farming landscapes. This approach not only preserves forests but also provides additional benefits such as shade, windbreaks, and carbon sequestration.

Water Conservation: One of the critical aspects of regenerative agriculture is its emphasis on water conservation. By implementing techniques like mulching, rainwater harvesting, and drip irrigation, farmers can significantly reduce water consumption while maintaining crop productivity. This not only conserves a precious resource but also enhances the durability of farming systems in the face of erratic weather patterns.

Climate tolerance: Climate change poses significant challenges to agriculture, including extreme weather events, shifting growing seasons, and increased pest pressure. Regenerative agriculture aims to enhance the resilience of agricultural systems to climate variability by improving soil structure, increasing organic matter content, and sequestering carbon in the soil.

Practices of Regenerative Agriculture:

Regenerative agriculture encompasses a wide range of practices designed to regenerate soil health, enhance biodiversity, and promote ecological balance. Some of the key practices include:

No-Till Farming: No-till or reduced tillage practices minimize soil disturbance by avoiding plowing or cultivating the soil. This helps preserve soil structure, reduce erosion, and enhance soil carbon sequestration.

Crop Rotation: Crop rotation involves alternating the types of crops grown on a piece of land over time. This practice helps break pest and disease cycles, improve soil fertility, and reduce the need for chemical inputs.

Agroforestry: Agroforestry integrates trees and shrubs into agricultural systems to provide multiple benefits, including shade, windbreaks, erosion control, and habitat for wildlife. Agroforestry systems can improve soil health, enhance biodiversity, and diversify farm income.

Cover Cropping: Cover cropping involves planting noncash crops during fallow periods to cover and protect the soil. Cover crops help reduce erosion, suppress weeds, improve soil structure, and add organic matter to the soil.

Importance of Soil Fertility: Nourishing the Roots of Crop Growth

Now, let's delve into the heart of agricultural productivity: soil fertility. Understanding the significance of soil fertility is paramount for cultivating thriving crops and sustaining healthy ecosystems. In this section, we'll explore how soil fertility directly influences crop growth, nutrient availability, and plant development, laying the groundwork for bountiful harvests and vibrant plantations.

The Key to Crop Growth

Soil fertility serves as the bedrock upon which successful crop growth is built. Fertile soils provide plants with the essential nutrients, water, and oxygen needed for vigorous growth and development. Nutrients such as nitrogen, phosphorus, and potassium play pivotal roles in various physiological processes, from photosynthesis and cell division to flower formation and fruit set. Moreover, fertile soils support a diverse community of beneficial microorganisms that aid in nutrient cycling, disease suppression, and soil structure improvement.

Meeting Crop Nutrient Requirements

Different crops have specific nutrient requirements at various growth stages, necessitating a balanced supply of essential elements for optimal performance. Nitrogen is vital for promoting vegetative growth and leafy green development; phosphorus supports root establishment and flowering, while potassium enhances overall plant vigor and disease resistance. Additionally, micronutrients such as iron, zinc, and manganese play critical roles in enzyme activation and metabolic processes, ensuring healthy plant growth and productivity. By maintaining soil fertility through organic amendments, cover cropping, and nutrient management practices, farmers can meet crop nutrient demands and maximize yields.

Nurturing Plantation Growth

Healthy soil fertility is synonymous with robust plantation growth, characterized by vigorous root development, lush foliage, and abundant fruiting. Adequate soil fertility supports the establishment of strong root systems, allowing plants to access water and nutrients efficiently while anchoring them firmly in the soil. Furthermore, fertile soils enhance nutrient uptake and assimilation, facilitating the synthesis of proteins, carbohydrates, and phytochemicals essential for plant growth, resilience, and productivity. By prioritizing soil health and fertility management, farmers can foster optimal plantation growth and ensure the long-term sustainability of their agricultural endeavors.

As stewards of the land, it's essential for us to recognize the invaluable role of soil fertility in supporting crop growth, nutrient cycling, and ecosystem resilience. By adopting regenerative practices that prioritize soil health and fertility enhancement, we can cultivate thriving crops, nourish our communities, and steward the land for generations to come.

Goals of Boosting Vegetable Yield and Optimizing Profits: Cultivating Success in Your Farm or Garden

As we conclude this introductory chapter, I want to share with you the inspiration behind writing this book and the profound impact that understanding soil health and regenerative agriculture has had on my own journey as a farmer.

Several years ago, I found myself facing a dilemma familiar to many farmers and gardeners: declining crop yields, soil degradation, and mounting input costs. Despite my best efforts and years of experience, I struggled to maintain productivity on my farm. Frustrated and disillusioned, I embarked on a quest to uncover the root causes of these challenges and find sustainable solutions.

It was during this journey that I stumbled upon the transformative principles of regenerative agriculture and the critical importance of soil health. One pivotal moment stands out vividly in my memory: while inspecting my fields, I noticed a stark contrast between the health and vitality of crops grown in well-nourished, biodiverse soils and those struggling in depleted compacted earth. It dawned on me that beneath the surface lies the key to unlocking the full potential of our agricultural endeavors.

Through years of experimentation, research, and collaboration with fellow farmers and agronomists, I came to realize that many of the prevailing notions about soil health and crop management were deeply flawed. Misconceptions about soil fertility, chemical inputs, and conventional farming practices had led us astray, compromising the health of our soils and the resilience of our farming systems.

This realization fueled my passion for sharing knowledge and empowering fellow farmers and gardeners to embrace regenerative practices that nurture the land and enrich our communities. By challenging conventional wisdom and embracing the principles of regenerative agriculture, we can cultivate abundance, restore ecosystem balance, and secure a prosperous future for generations to come.

As we embark on this journey together, my goal is to provide you with practical insights, actionable strategies, and evidence-based guidance to boost vegetable yields, optimize profits, and steward the land with care and respect. From precision agriculture techniques to integrated pest management strategies, we'll explore a myriad of approaches to enhance crop productivity, resource efficiency, and farm profitability.

1. **Different Ways of Optimizing Vegetable Crops:** Explore innovative techniques such as companion planting, crop rotation, and intercropping to maximize yields and minimize pest and disease pressure.
2. **Types of Emplacements and Better Management Plans:** Learn how to design efficient farm layouts, implement effective irrigation systems, and integrate agroforestry practices to optimize space utilization and resource allocation.
3. **Practice Precision Agriculture:** Dive into the world of precision agriculture, utilizing technologies like drones, sensors, and data analytics to optimize input applications, monitor crop health, and enhance decision-making for improved productivity and profitability.
4. **Optimizing Irrigation and Managing Pests and Diseases:** Discover strategies for optimizing irrigation schedules, implementing water-saving techniques, and adopting holistic approaches to pest and disease management, reducing reliance on synthetic inputs and promoting ecological balance.
5. **Comprehensive Crop Management Plans:** Develop comprehensive crop management plans tailored to your farm

or garden, incorporating soil health assessments, nutrient management strategies, and crop rotation schedules to maximize productivity, minimize environmental impact, and optimize profits.

Join me in the chapters ahead as we dig deeper into the details of soil fertility, crop management, and profit optimization, unlocking the secrets to sustainable success in farming and gardening.

Chapter One — From the Earthy Depths to Fertile Ground: Understanding Your Soil

Soil, often termed as the skin of the Earth, is more than just a medium in which plants grow; it is a vibrant, living ecosystem vital for the sustainability of life. The history of soil health assessment stretches back millennia, deeply rooted in the very inception of agriculture.

Ancient civilizations, though lacking modern scientific tools, had an astute awareness of the significance of fertile soil. The Nile Valley, for instance, was the breadbasket of the ancient world, its fertility renowned, owing to the nutrient-rich sediments deposited by the annual flooding of the Nile. Similarly, the Mesopotamians, with their intricate irrigation systems, demonstrated an early understanding of managing soil for crop production.

The true scientific study of soil, however, began to take shape in the 19th century. Justus von Liebig, a German chemist, is often credited as the father of soil chemistry. His work in the mid-1800s, which emphasized the role of mineral nutrients in plant growth, revolutionized the way we perceive soil fertility. Liebig's law of the minimum states that plant growth is not limited by the total amount of resources available but by the scarcest resource. This principle laid the foundation for modern agricultural science, pivoting the focus toward understanding and managing soil nutrients.

Following Liebig, scientists like Friedrich Fallou began to classify soils based on their physical and chemical properties, leading to the birth of pedology (the study of soils in their natural environment). These early works were pivotal in transforming soil assessment from an art practiced by farmers to a science that could be studied and improved upon.

By the early 20th century, soil science had evolved considerably. The Dust Bowl of the 1930s in the United States brought the importance of soil conservation to the forefront. This period of severe dust storms dramatically demonstrated the consequences of poor agricultural practices. It led to the establishment of the Soil Conservation Service in 1935 (now the Natural Resources Conservation Service). This marked a shift in soil science, from focusing solely on soil fertility to understanding soil as a dynamic, living system that needed to be conserved and managed sustainably.

Today, soil health assessment is not just about measuring nutrient levels and pH. It's about understanding soil as a complex system that includes physical, chemical, and biological components. The health of soil is now viewed in the context of its capacity to function as a living ecosystem, sustaining plants, animals, and humans.

As we delve deeper into this chapter, we will explore the various aspects of soil health, starting with the critical factors that determine soil performance and function. We'll look at how these factors interact with each other and with the environment to influence plant growth and crop yield. This understanding is crucial for anyone looking to cultivate the land, be it a small-scale home gardener or a large-scale farmer.

In the following sections, we will also explore the principles of soil health assessment. This includes understanding the role of soil structure and composition, the importance of soil biology and microorganisms, and the need for soil conservation and management. We'll provide practical tips and advice grounded in scientific theory to help you assess and improve the health of your soil.

Understanding soil health is a journey — one that starts with the basics of soil science and leads to a deeper appreciation of the land beneath our feet. As we embark on this journey together, remember that healthy soil is not just about growing plants; it's about sustaining life on Earth. Let's begin by delving into the factors that are considered in soil performance and function.

Soil Health Assessment

Factors in Soil Performance and Function

Soil, a complex and dynamic entity, is more than just dirt beneath our feet. It's a living, breathing ecosystem that plays a crucial role in supporting life on Earth. To understand and assess soil health effectively, one must consider its multifaceted nature, which includes physical, chemical, and biological components.

Physical Aspect: The physical properties of soil, primarily texture and structure, are fundamental in determining its health. Soil texture refers to the proportion of different-sized particles — sand, silt, and clay. This composition affects a soil's drainage and aeration capabilities. Sandy soils, for instance, have large particles and high porosity, leading to quick water drainage but poor nutrient retention. Clay soils, on the other hand, with their fine particles, retain water and nutrients well but may suffer from poor aeration and drainage.

Soil structure describes how these particles are aggregated. Good soil structure is essential for supporting plant growth, as it influences root penetration, water infiltration, and air movement within the soil. It also impacts the soil's capacity to hold and supply water and nutrients to plants.

Chemical Aspect: Chemically, soil health is often gauged by its pH and nutrient content. Soil pH, the measure of acidity or alkalinity, significantly affects nutrient availability to plants. Most nutrients are readily available in slightly acidic to neutral soils (pH 6-7). Soil fertility, another chemical attribute, hinges on the presence of essential nutrients like nitrogen, phosphorus, and potassium. The balance of these nutrients is critical; an excess or deficiency can lead to poor plant health and reduced yields.

Biological Aspect: The biological component, often the most overlooked aspect of soil health, includes the myriad of microorganisms present in the soil — bacteria, fungi, protozoa, nematodes, and more. These microorganisms play a pivotal role in nutrient cycling, organic matter decomposition, and the formation of soil structure. They are also crucial in suppressing soil-borne diseases and promoting plant growth.

These physical, chemical, and biological components are deeply interconnected. For instance, soil structure affects water retention, which in turn influences the soil's chemical properties like nutrient solubility. Similarly, the biological activity in soil is influenced by its physical and chemical conditions. A healthy soil is one where these components are in balance, creating an environment conducive to plant growth.

Crop, Yield, Water Quality, and Weather Conditions

The health of soil directly translates into the health and yield of crops grown in it. Healthy soil provides a supportive environment for roots, ensuring adequate water and nutrient uptake. This leads to robust plant growth and higher crop yields. Conversely, poor soil health can lead to weak root systems, inadequate nutrient uptake, and, ultimately, reduced plant vigor and crop yield.

Soil health also has a profound impact on water quality. Healthy soil has good structure and organic matter content, which allows it to effectively filter and store water. This reduces runoff, preventing soil erosion and the leaching of nutrients and pollutants into water bodies. Moreover, well-structured soil helps in maintaining water balance in the landscape, reducing the impact of both droughts and floods.

The influence of weather and climate on soil conditions cannot be overstated. Extreme weather events, like heavy rains or prolonged droughts, can severely affect soil health. Heavy rains can lead to erosion and nutrient runoff in soils lacking proper structure, while droughts can deplete soil moisture, affecting its biological activity and nutrient cycling. Climate change, with its propensity for increasing the frequency and intensity of such extreme weather events, poses a significant challenge to maintaining soil health.

In the subsequent sections, we will delve deeper into the principles of soil health assessment and explore practical ways to test and improve the health of your soil. Understanding and managing these complex interactions within the soil is key to sustainable agriculture and a healthier planet.

Principles of Soil Health Assessment

Fundamental Principle of Soil Health Assessment

Understanding soil as a living, dynamic system is crucial. Soil isn't just an inert growing medium but a vibrant ecosystem. Studies estimate that a single teaspoon of healthy soil can contain up to one billion bacteria, several yards of fungal filaments, several thousand protozoa, and scores of nematodes. These microorganisms are essential for nutrient cycling and maintaining soil health.

Understanding the Role of Soil Structure and Composition

Soil structure refers to the arrangement of soil particles into groups called aggregates. These aggregates are essential for good water infiltration and air circulation. Research shows that well-structured soil can reduce erosion rates by up to 20-33% compared to poorly structured soil. Soil composition also matters significantly; for instance, sandy soils are typically low in nutrient content but high in drainage capacity.

The Importance of Soil Biology and Microorganisms

Soil biology is a critical component of soil health. A diverse microbial population helps decompose organic matter, fix nitrogen, control soil-borne diseases, and support plant growth. Fascinatingly, a single gram of soil can contain up to 10,000 different species of bacteria. These microorganisms form symbiotic relationships with plants, such as mycorrhizal associations, which are crucial for nutrient absorption.

Emphasis on Soil Nutrient Balance

Balancing soil nutrients is more complex than just applying fertilizers. It involves understanding the soil's natural nutrient cycle and its capacity to retain and release nutrients. For instance, excessive use of nitrogenous fertilizers can lead to soil acidification and nutrient leaching, affecting both soil health and water quality. Nutrient balance is also about the right proportion of macronutrients (nitrogen, phosphorus, potassium) and micronutrients (such as zinc, copper, and iron), which are equally crucial for plant health.

Integrating Soil Conservation and Management

Conservation practices like crop rotation, cover cropping, and reduced tillage have significant impacts on soil health. For example, studies have shown that crop rotation can increase soil organic matter content by up to 10%. Cover crops, such as legumes, can fix atmospheric nitrogen in the soil, reducing the need for synthetic fertilizers. Reduced or no-till farming practices help preserve soil structure, reduce erosion, and enhance water retention.

A holistic approach to soil health recognizes the interconnectedness of these principles. It's not enough to focus on just one aspect, such as nutrient levels or pH balance. Effective soil health management requires an understanding of how physical, chemical and biological factors interact and influence each other.

This holistic approach also acknowledges the impact of human activities and environmental factors on soil health. It demands adaptive management practices that respond to ongoing changes in soil conditions due to factors like weather patterns, crop choices, and land use changes.

In summary, the principles of soil health assessment underline the need to view soil as a living, breathing ecosystem that requires balance and care. By adhering to these principles, farmers and gardeners can enhance soil functionality, support sustainable agriculture, and contribute to the overall health of our planet. The next sections will delve into practical methods for testing soil health and managing it sustainably, reinforcing these principles in action.

Testing Soil Health in the Field

Testing soil health is a critical step in understanding and managing the land for agricultural or gardening purposes. Several common field tests can be conducted to assess soil texture, structure, pH, nutrient content, and biological activity. Understanding how to interpret these test results is key to making informed decisions for soil management.

Soil Texture Test

Soil texture, determined by the proportion of sand, silt, and clay, can be assessed using the feel method. This involves moistening a soil sample and rolling it in your hands to form a ball, then trying to form a ribbon. Sandy soils feel gritty and won't form a ribbon; silty soils feel smooth; clay soils feel sticky and can form a long ribbon. Texture influences water retention and nutrient availability. For example, sandy soils drain quickly but don't hold nutrients well, while clay soils retain water and nutrients but may have poor drainage.

Soil Structure Assessment

Soil structure is observed by examining the soil's aggregation. Healthy soil should have distinct, well-formed aggregates that are neither too loose nor too compact. Compacted soil indicates poor structure, which can impede root growth and reduce air and water infiltration. Conversely, well-aggregated soil provides ideal conditions for root development and efficient water and nutrient movement.

Soil pH Test

Soil pH can be measured using a simple pH test kit or a digital pH meter. The pH scale ranges from 0 to 14, with 7 being neutral. Soils with a pH lower than 6 are acidic, and those above 7 are alkaline. Most plants prefer a slightly acidic to neutral pH (6-7). Acidic soils may require liming to raise the pH, while alkaline soils might benefit from sulfur additions to lower the pH.

Nutrient Content Analysis

Field kits are available for testing primary nutrients like nitrogen, phosphorus, and potassium. These tests typically involve adding a soil sample to a chemical solution and comparing the color change to a standard chart. For a more detailed analysis, soil samples can be sent to a laboratory. High nutrient levels may indicate over-fertilization, risking nutrient runoff and leaching, while low levels could lead to poor plant growth.

Biological Activity Test

Biological activity in soil can be assessed by observing earthworm activity. Simply count the number of earthworms in a specific volume of soil (e.g., one cubic foot). A healthy soil should have at least 10-15 earthworms in this volume. Earthworm presence indicates a well-aerated, nutrient-rich soil. Other tests include measuring microbial biomass or observing the rate of organic matter decomposition.

Interpreting Test Results

Understanding what these test results infer is crucial. For instance:

- A predominantly sandy soil indicates the need for regular organic matter additions to improve nutrient and water retention.
- Compacted soil suggests the necessity for aeration or reduced tillage practices.
- A pH significantly out of the ideal range for your crops may necessitate amendments to correct it.
- Imbalanced nutrient levels can be addressed through tailored fertilization strategies.
- Low biological activity might indicate the need for organic amendments to boost microbial populations.

Each of these parameters offers insight into the current state of the soil and guides what actions are needed to improve its health and productivity. Regular testing allows for monitoring changes over time and adjusting management practices accordingly. Remember, the goal is to create a balanced soil environment that supports healthy plant growth while maintaining or enhancing soil health.

The 4'R's of Soil Assessment

In the realm of soil health and fertility management, the concept of the 4'R's plays a pivotal role. This framework revolves around using the Right source at the Right rate, at the Right time, and in the Right place. Adhering to these principles not only ensures optimal plant growth and yield but also minimizes environmental impacts and enhances soil health.

Right Source

Choosing the right source of nutrients involves selecting appropriate fertilizers or amendments that meet the specific nutrient requirements of the soil and the crops being grown. This means understanding both the soil's existing nutrient profile and the specific needs of the plants. For instance, a soil deficient in nitrogen may benefit from a nitrogen-rich amendment, while one low in phosphorus would require a different approach.

Right Rate

Applying nutrients at the right rate is crucial to avoid under or over-fertilization. Under-fertilization can lead to poor crop growth and yield, while over-fertilization can cause nutrient runoff into water bodies, leading to environmental issues like eutrophication. The right rate should be determined based on soil test results, crop nutrient requirements, and considering any residual nutrients already present in the soil.

Right Time

Timing the application of nutrients is essential for plants to maximize their uptake and minimize losses due to leaching or volatilization. For example, applying nitrogen just before heavy rain is likely to result in significant leaching, while applying it when the crop can readily utilize it ensures maximum benefit. Understanding the crop growth stages and their nutrient uptake patterns is key to determining the right timing.

Right Place

The placement of nutrients is as important as the timing. Nutrients need to be applied so that the plants can easily access them. This could mean incorporating fertilizers into the soil, applying them as a top dressing, or using foliar applications. Placement decisions should consider the mobility of the nutrient in the soil (e.g., phosphorus is relatively immobile and should be placed close to the plant roots) and the root architecture of the crop.

Impact on Soil Management Decisions

The 4'R's framework guides informed soil management decisions. It encourages a holistic view of nutrient management, emphasizing efficiency and sustainability. By following these principles, farmers and gardeners can achieve optimal crop performance while protecting the soil ecosystem and the wider environment. This approach not only improves current crop yields but also ensures the long-term health and productivity of the soil, which is essential for sustainable agriculture.

Building Sustainable Topsoil

After understanding soil health and the principles guiding its assessment, the focus shifts to practical strategies for building and maintaining sustainable topsoil. This section explores key practices like composting, cover cropping, and crop rotation, including real-world case studies demonstrating their successful application.

Composting

Composting is the process of converting organic waste into a rich soil amendment, known as compost. This practice is essential for improving soil structure, increasing organic matter content, and enhancing microbial activity. By adding compost to the soil, farmers and gardeners can improve water retention, nutrient availability, and overall soil fertility. A study from Cornell University highlighted that regular compost application could increase soil organic matter by up to 30% within a few years, significantly enhancing soil health.

Cover Cropping

Cover crops are planted not for harvest but to cover the soil, thereby improving its quality and fertility. They help reduce soil erosion, suppress weeds, enhance soil moisture, and improve biodiversity. Leguminous cover crops, such as clover and vetch, are particularly beneficial as they fix nitrogen in the soil, reducing the need for synthetic fertilizers. A case study from the Rodale Institute demonstrated that using cover crops could increase soil organic carbon by 8.9 metric tons per hectare over a decade, showcasing their impact on soil health.

Crop Rotation

Crop rotation involves alternating the types of crops grown in a particular area across different seasons or years. This practice prevents the depletion of specific nutrients, reduces the buildup of pests and diseases, and can improve soil structure and fertility. For instance, a study by the USDA found that rotating corn with soybeans and wheat not only reduced the need for chemical inputs but also led to a 10% increase in corn yield compared to continuous corn cultivation.

Case Studies of Successful Topsoil Improvement

Organic Farming in Denmark: A Danish farm shifted from conventional to organic farming, implementing practices like composting and crop rotation. Over 20 years, they reported a significant improvement in soil organic matter and a noticeable increase in yields, demonstrating the long-term benefits of sustainable soil management practices.

No-Till Farming in the U.S.: In the United States, a farm adopted no-till farming combined with cover cropping. This approach resulted in a 15% increase in topsoil depth over 25 years and a substantial improvement in soil water retention and nutrient cycling.

Urban Composting in Toronto, Canada: In Toronto, a city-wide composting program was initiated where organic household waste is collected and processed into compost. This compost is then made available to local gardeners and farmers. Reports indicated a notable improvement in urban garden yields and soil quality, highlighting the impact of community-level composting initiatives on urban agriculture.

Diversified Farming in Iowa, USA: An Iowa farm integrated cover crops like rye and clover into their corn-soybean rotation. This led to a 25% reduction in soil erosion and a noticeable improvement in soil organic matter, demonstrating the effectiveness of cover crops in diverse cropping systems.

Sustainable Agriculture in Kenya: In a region of Kenya, smallholder farmers adopted a rotation system involving maize, beans, and cover crops. This practice led to a 20% increase in maize yields and improved soil health, showcasing the benefits of crop rotation in enhancing agricultural sustainability in challenging environments.

Identifying Different Soil Types

Understanding and identifying different soil types are crucial for effective soil management. The characteristics of soil, such as texture, color, and composition, greatly influence its water retention, nutrient availability, and suitability for plant growth. Here's a guide to help identify common soil types and understand their implications for gardening and farming.

Soil Texture

Soil texture is determined by the size of the particles that make up the soil. The three main types of soil particles are sand, silt, and clay, and the combination of these particles gives soil its texture.

- **Sandy Soil:** Feels gritty. Large particles with spacious gaps. Sandy soils drain quickly but don't hold nutrients well.
- **Silty Soil:** Feels smooth, like flour. Smaller particles than sand but larger than clay. Silty soils have better nutrient retention and water-holding capacity than sandy soils.
- **Clay Soil:** Feels sticky when wet. Very small particles with little space between them. Clay soils are nutrient-rich but have poor drainage and aeration.

Soil Color

The color of soil can provide information about its organic matter content and drainage characteristics.

- **Dark Soil:** Rich in organic matter, typically indicating good fertility.
- **Red or Orange Soil:** High in iron oxide, often found in well-drained areas.
- **Light Brown or Yellow Soil:** May indicate lower organic matter and poor drainage.

Composition and Structure

Soil composition refers to the makeup of the soil in terms of organic and inorganic materials, while structure relates to how these particles are arranged or clumped together.

- **Loamy Soil:** A balanced mixture of sand, silt, clay, and organic matter. Considered ideal for most plants due to its balance of drainage and nutrient retention.
- **Peaty Soil:** High organic matter content, typically dark and damp. Good for growth but may need nutrients added.
- **Chalky Soil:** Contains larger particles with a higher pH level. It may require added nutrients and organic matter to support plant growth.

Impact on Water Retention, Nutrient Availability, and Plant Growth

- **Sandy Soil:** Quick drainage can lead to frequent water and nutrient needs. Suitable for plants that prefer dry conditions.
- **Silty Soil:** Better at holding water and nutrients than sandy soil, supporting a wider range of plants.
- **Clay Soil:** Tends to retain water and nutrients but may become waterlogged, hampering root growth. Ideal for moisture-loving plants but may need amendments to improve drainage.
- **Loamy Soil:** Often ideal for most plants, providing a balance of moisture retention and nutrient availability.
- **Peaty Soil:** Excellent for retaining moisture but may require additional nutrients.
- **Chalky Soil:** Can lead to stunted plant growth due to nutrient deficiencies, especially in acid-loving plants. Often requires fertilization and organic matter additions.

Understanding these soil types and their characteristics can guide gardeners and farmers in choosing the right plants for their soil type or modifying the soil to suit specific plant requirements. Soil testing for pH and nutrient content can further aid in tailoring soil management practices for optimal plant growth and soil health.

Nutrient Analysis

Nutrient analysis of soil is pivotal for effective soil management, allowing for the precise application of fertilizers and amendments. Understanding the nutrient content helps address deficiencies, avoid excesses, and ensure optimal plant growth. Here's an overview of methodologies for determining nutrient content in soils and the relevance of this analysis in soil management.

Methodologies for Determining Soil Nutrient Content

- **Soil Sampling:** The first step is to collect soil samples from different locations and depths within the plot to get a representative sample. This is crucial for accurate analysis.
- **Laboratory Testing:** The most comprehensive method for nutrient analysis. Soil samples are sent to a laboratory where they are tested for a range of nutrients, including nitrogen (N), phosphorus (P), potassium (K), calcium (Ca), magnesium (Mg),

sulfur (S), and micronutrients like iron (Fe), manganese (Mn), copper (Cu), and zinc (Zn).
- o **Chemical Extraction:** Various chemicals are used to extract nutrients from the soil, which are then measured using spectrometry or chromatography.
- o **pH Testing:** Measures the acidity or alkalinity of the soil, which affects nutrient availability.
- **Field Kits and Portable Devices:** Provide an immediate, albeit less comprehensive, analysis. They often include colorimetric tests for specific nutrients.
- **Soil Test Meters:** Handheld devices that can measure pH, moisture content, and sometimes specific nutrients directly in the field.
- **Remote Sensing Technologies:** Advanced technologies using drones or satellites can assess soil conditions over large areas, though they are less precise for specific nutrient measurements.

Relevance of Nutrient Analysis in Soil Management

- **Tailored Fertilization:** Knowing the specific nutrient makeup of soil allows for customized fertilizer application. This prevents overuse or underuse of fertilizers, promoting cost-effective and environmentally friendly farming.
- **Identifying Deficiencies and Toxicities:** Nutrient analysis can pinpoint specific deficiencies or toxicities in the soil. For example, a nitrogen deficiency might manifest in stunted growth and pale green leaves. In contrast, excess nitrogen can lead to excessive foliage growth at the expense of fruit or flower development.

- **pH Adjustment:** Understanding soil pH is crucial since it affects nutrient availability. Certain nutrients become unavailable to plants if the pH is too high or too low.
- **Monitoring Soil Health Over Time:** Regular nutrient analysis helps track changes in soil health, especially after amendments or changing cultivation practices are applied.
- **Supporting Sustainable Practices:** Accurate nutrient analysis supports sustainable soil management by ensuring that only the necessary amount of inputs is applied, reducing runoff and environmental impact.

In summary, nutrient analysis is a key component of informed soil management. It guides farmers and gardeners in making data-driven decisions to maintain balanced soil health, optimize plant growth, and contribute to sustainable agricultural practices.

Techniques for Identifying Soil Types

Identifying soil types is crucial for effective land management, and advancements in technology have introduced sophisticated methods like soil spectroscopy and remote sensing. These techniques complement traditional methods, offering detailed insights into soil composition and condition. Let's explore these advanced techniques along with their advantages and disadvantages.

Soil Spectroscopy

Soil spectroscopy involves analyzing the reflectance of soil in various wavelengths of light to determine its properties.

Pros:

- **High Precision:** Provides detailed information about soil composition, including organic matter content, mineralogy, and moisture levels.
- **Rapid Analysis:** Offers quick results compared to traditional lab-based tests.
- **Non-Destructive:** Doesn't alter or harm the soil sample.

Cons:

- **Cost:** The equipment for soil spectroscopy can be expensive.
- **Expertise Required:** Interpretation of spectroscopy data typically requires specialized knowledge.
- **Limited by Soil Conditions:** Accuracy can be affected by soil moisture, texture, and surface roughness.

Remote Sensing

Remote sensing involves using satellite or aerial imagery to assess soil characteristics over large areas.

Pros:

- **Large Area Coverage:** Capable of analyzing vast tracts of land, which is beneficial for large-scale farming or land management.
- **Versatility:** Useful for a range of applications, including soil type classification, moisture content assessment, and crop monitoring.
- **Temporal Analysis:** Allows for monitoring changes in soil over time.

Cons:

- **Resolution Limitations**: The level of detail can be limited depending on the sensor's resolution.
- **Weather Dependent:** Cloud cover and weather conditions can impact the quality of imagery.
- **Data Interpretation:** Requires sophisticated software and expertise for analysis.

While advanced techniques like soil spectroscopy and remote sensing offer detailed soil analysis, they may not be feasible for small-scale farmers due to cost and technical requirements. However, small-scale farmers have access to practical, low-cost methods for identifying soil types that can significantly aid in effective soil management. Here's how they can assess their soil using accessible techniques.

Soil Texture by Feel Method

This is a hands-on approach to determine the soil texture — whether it's sandy, silty, or clayey.

- **Procedure:** Wet a small amount of soil and try to form a ball. Then, attempt to roll it into a thin ribbon. The ease with which you can form a ribbon and its length helps determine the soil type.
- **Interpretation:** If the soil forms a ribbon easily and it's quite long before it breaks, it likely has a high clay content.
  - If it forms a short ribbon, it has a more balanced mix (loamy).
  - If it falls apart before forming a ribbon, it's likely sandy.

Jar Test for Soil Composition

This test provides a visual representation of the soil composition.

- **Procedure:** Fill a clear jar about halfway with soil, add water, shake well, and let it settle for a day or two.
- **Interpretation:** The layers that settle will show sand at the bottom, then silt and clay on top. The thickness of each layer gives an idea of the soil composition.

Basic pH Testing

Soil pH can be tested using affordable kits available at garden stores.

- **Procedure:** Follow the kit instructions, usually involving mixing soil with a chemical and comparing the color change to a pH chart.

- **Interpretation:** This test indicates if the soil is acidic, neutral, or alkaline, which is critical for deciding on suitable crops or necessary amendments.

Observing Plant Indicators and Weeds

The types of plants and weeds that thrive in your soil can also indicate soil type and health.

- **Procedure:** Observe the types of weeds and plants that naturally grow in your soil.
- **Interpretation:** Certain plants prefer specific soil types; for example, dandelions indicate acidic soil, while chickweed suggests fertile soil.

Choosing the Right Technique

The choice of technique depends on factors like the scale of the land, specific information required, available resources, and expertise. Large-scale operations or detailed soil assessments might benefit from advanced techniques like spectroscopy or remote sensing, while traditional methods are suitable for small-scale, immediate assessments. Often, a combination of methods provides the most comprehensive understanding of soil types and conditions.

Incorporating these techniques into soil management practices allows for more precise and informed decision-making, ultimately leading to better soil health and more efficient agricultural practices.

As we conclude this chapter, it's important to reflect on the central theme that has emerged: the soil is not just a substrate for plant growth but a dynamic, living ecosystem that demands our understanding and respect.

In summary, this chapter serves as a foundation for understanding the complexity and beauty of the soil beneath our feet. Whether you're a seasoned farmer or a beginner gardener, the journey to healthy soil is continuous and ever-evolving. By embracing the principles and practices outlined in this chapter, you are not just growing plants; you are cultivating an ecosystem, contributing to the health of our planet, and participating in the ancient and noble art of agriculture. Remember, every step taken to improve soil health is a step toward a more sustainable and fruitful relationship with the earth.

Chapter Two — Building Soil Health (Part I)

Soil fertility, the cornerstone of agriculture, underpins the vast panorama of food production that sustains human civilizations. This pivotal concept is not merely about the richness of the earth beneath our feet. However, it encompasses an intricate tapestry of biological, chemical, and physical properties that make soil not just a medium for plant growth but a living, breathing ecosystem in its own right.

Overview of Soil Fertility

Soil fertility is a measure of how well soil can support plant growth. It's influenced by a variety of factors, including the presence of essential nutrients, soil structure, water availability, pH levels, and microbial activity. Nutrients like nitrogen, phosphorus, and potassium are the most well-known, but micronutrients such as iron, manganese, and zinc are equally crucial, albeit required in smaller quantities.

Soil structure, referring to the arrangement of soil particles, significantly impacts water retention, drainage, and aeration — all vital for root development and health. Microbial activity, often less visible but immensely influential, involves the complex interplay of bacteria, fungi, and other microorganisms that contribute to nutrient cycling, organic matter decomposition, and soil structure maintenance.

In a world where soil degradation is becoming increasingly prevalent due to unsustainable agricultural practices, understanding and enhancing soil fertility is not just an academic pursuit but a necessity for future food security.

Importance of Sustainable Practices in Agriculture

Sustainable agricultural practices are fundamental in maintaining and enhancing soil fertility. The essence of sustainability in agriculture lies in balancing the immediate needs for crop production with the long-term health of the soil ecosystem. Such practices aim to minimize environmental impact, reduce reliance on chemical inputs, and promote biodiversity.

One of the most pressing reasons to adopt sustainable methods is soil erosion. This process strips the nutrient-rich upper layer of soil, leaving behind a less fertile, compacted substrate. Soil erosion, driven by wind and water, is exacerbated by practices such as over-tilling, deforestation, and inappropriate irrigation methods.

Moreover, the overuse of chemical fertilizers, while providing short-term boosts in productivity, can lead to soil acidification, disruption of microbial communities, and nutrient imbalances. These issues not only degrade soil quality but can also contribute to water pollution and greenhouse gas emissions.

In response, sustainable practices such as cover cropping, crop rotation, composting, and the use of natural fertilizers have emerged as key strategies. These methods help restore soil health, increase organic matter content, improve soil structure, and enhance the biodiversity of soil organisms. They create a symbiotic relationship between farming and the natural environment, where each benefits the other.

For instance, cover crops, when grown in the off-season or alongside main crops, protect the soil from erosion, improve its organic matter content, and can even fix atmospheric nitrogen in the soil. Crop rotation is the practice of growing different types of crops in the same area across a sequence of growing seasons, breaking pest and disease cycles and balancing nutrient demands on the soil.

Composting is a process of recycling organic material like plant remains and kitchen scraps into rich soil amendments, which is beneficial for improving soil structure and nutrient content. Natural fertilizers, derived from plant or animal sources, supply essential nutrients without the adverse environmental impacts associated with their synthetic counterparts.

In conclusion, this chapter aims to delve deep into these sustainable practices, unraveling their mechanisms, benefits, and methods of application in the realm of modern agriculture. By understanding and implementing these practices, we can ensure the fertility of our soils and the sustainability of our agricultural systems for generations to come.

Cover Cropping Strategies

Definition and Purpose of Cover Cropping

Cover cropping is an agronomic practice involving the growth of specific plants not primarily intended for harvest but for benefiting the soil and subsequent crops. The purpose of cover cropping extends beyond mere soil coverage; it encompasses soil health enhancement, moisture conservation, weed management, pest and disease control, and biodiversity promotion.

Historical Implementation of Cover Cropping

1. **Traditional Methods** — Traditionally, farmers around the world employed cover crops as a means of

maintaining soil fertility and structure. Ancient civilizations, like the Romans and Greeks, used legumes to enrich the soil. These traditional methods were based on the observation of natural ecosystems where soil was seldom left bare.
2. **Modern Adaptations** — In the modern era, cover cropping evolved with the advancement of agricultural science. Research provided data on specific benefits, such as nitrogen fixation by legumes, leading to a more targeted and efficient use of cover crops. Today, farmers integrate cover crops into crop rotations and conservation tillage systems.

Various Methods of Cover Cropping

1. **Winter Cover Cropping** — Utilized in colder climates, winter cover crops like cereal rye or hairy vetch are sown in the fall and grow through the winter. These crops prevent nutrient leaching and soil erosion during winter months when fields might otherwise be bare. They also provide organic matter, enhancing soil structure and fertility for spring-planted crops.
2. **Green Manure** — Green manure, a type of cover crop such as clover or alfalfa, is planted to be tilled back into the soil. It's particularly effective in adding organic matter and nutrients, especially nitrogen, back into the soil. For instance, legumes can fix atmospheric nitrogen, reducing the need for synthetic fertilizers.
3. **Intercropping** — This involves growing cover crops alongside or between rows of cash crops.

Intercropping maximizes land use efficiency and promotes a diverse ecosystem. It can lead to reduced pest and disease outbreaks and improved soil conditions, as different plants contribute differently to soil health.

4. **Living Mulches** — These are low-growing cover crops that are planted with or around main crops and serve as mulch. They suppress weeds, help maintain soil moisture, and reduce temperature fluctuations. Living mulches also support beneficial insects and can reduce soil compaction.

5. **Relay Cropping** — Relay cropping involves planting a cover crop in a standing cash crop before its harvest. This ensures immediate soil coverage post-harvest. An example is planting clover in winter wheat in the spring. Clover continues to grow after wheat is harvested, providing continuous soil coverage and nitrogen fixation.

6. **Catch Crops** — Catch crops are fast-growing crops planted between regular production crops. Their purpose is to 'catch' nutrients that might otherwise leach away, particularly in times of heavy rainfall. An example is the use of mustard as a catch crop, which is known for its rapid growth and ability to uptake excess nitrogen.

Benefits of Cover Cropping

1. **Soil Erosion Prevention** — Cover crops protect the soil from wind and water erosion. Their roots stabilize the soil, and their foliage intercepts rain, reducing the force of impact on the soil. The USDA's Natural

Resources Conservation Service reports that cover cropping can significantly reduce soil erosion, sometimes by more than 50%.

2. **Enhancement of Soil Structure** — The root systems of cover crops improve soil structure by creating channels for air and water movement, enhancing root penetration for subsequent crops. A study by the Rodale Institute showed that cover crops like annual ryegrass and oats significantly improve soil porosity and aggregate stability.

3. **Nutrient Management** — Cover crops assist in nutrient cycling within the soil ecosystem. They can absorb excess nutrients, such as nitrates, and store them in their biomass. Upon decomposition, these nutrients are slowly released back into the soil, becoming available for future crops. This process is particularly crucial for preventing nitrate leaching into waterways.

4. **Weed Suppression** — Cover crops can outcompete weeds for resources such as light, nutrients, and water, effectively suppressing weed growth. For example, a dense cover crop like cereal rye creates a canopy that shades out potential weed seedlings, reducing weed pressure in subsequent crops.

5. **Enhancing Water Infiltration and Retention** — Cover crops improve soil's ability to absorb and hold water, reducing runoff and increasing drought resilience. Their root systems create channels in the soil, enhancing infiltration. A study by Penn State University found that fields with cover crops had

improved water infiltration rates compared to those without.
6. **Supporting Beneficial Soil Organisms** — Diverse cover crops provide a habitat and food source for beneficial soil organisms, including earthworms, beneficial nematodes, and a variety of microbes. These organisms play a crucial role in nutrient cycling, organic matter breakdown, and improving soil structure and health.
7. **Carbon Sequestration** — By growing and incorporating biomass into the soil, cover crops sequester carbon, mitigating climate change. The roots of cover crops are particularly important in this regard, as they deposit organic carbon deep into the soil profile.

Selection of Cover Crops

1. Criteria for Choosing Cover Crops

The choice of a cover crop hinges on multiple factors, each playing a significant role in achieving specific agricultural objectives:

- **Soil Improvement Goals:** If the primary goal is to enhance soil organic matter, crops like sorghum-sudangrass, known for high biomass production, are ideal. For nitrogen fixation, legumes such as clovers and vetches are preferred.
- **Soil Structure Enhancement:** Deep-rooted crops like radishes are chosen for breaking up compact soil and improving aeration and water infiltration.

- **Crop Rotation Compatibility:** The cover crop should complement the main crop rotation, either by adding missing nutrients back into the soil or by helping manage soil-borne diseases and pests.

2. Best Cover Crops for Different Soil Types

- **Sandy Soils:** Sandy soils benefit from crops like daikon radishes and sunflowers, which have deep roots that penetrate the soil, improving structure and nutrient accessibility. Their roots help in breaking up hardpans and bring nutrients from deeper layers to the surface.
- **Clay Soils:** In dense clay soils, crops such as crimson clover and ryegrass are beneficial. Their roots penetrate the heavy soil, improving aeration and drainage. These crops also contribute organic matter, enhancing soil texture and fertility over time.

3. Regional Variations in Cover Crop Selection

Regional climate significantly influences the choice of cover crops:

- **Cooler Northern Climates:** Winter-hardy crops like winter rye and hairy vetch are effective. They can survive harsh winters and provide early spring growth, which is crucial for protecting and nourishing the soil in cold regions.
- **Warmer Southern Climates:** Heat and drought-tolerant crops like cowpeas and sorghum-sudangrass are suitable. They thrive in hot

climates and are resistant to dry conditions, making them ideal for southern regions.

4. Climate Adaptation

Adapting cover crop selection to local climatic conditions is vital:

- **Drought-prone Areas:** Drought-tolerant species such as cowpeas and buckwheat are preferred. These crops can withstand water scarcity and still provide soil coverage and benefits.
- **Cooler, Wetter Climates:** Species like ryegrass or clover, which thrive in cooler and moister conditions, are ideal for such climates. They can survive and grow effectively in lower temperatures and higher moisture levels.

5. Pest and Disease Considerations

Cover crops can play a significant role in pest and disease management:

- **Nematode Suppression:** Marigolds are known for their ability to suppress nematodes, a common soil pest.
- **Biofumigation:** Mustard plants can act as biofumigants. When incorporated into the soil, they release compounds that reduce soil-borne diseases, benefiting subsequent crops.

6. Economic and Operational Factors

Practicality and economics also guide cover crop selection:

- **Cost-Effectiveness:** The cost of seeds and their availability can influence choices. Farmers often opt for affordable and readily available options.
- **Ease of Incorporation and Termination:** The ability to easily incorporate and terminate cover crops is crucial, especially in no-till farming systems. For instance, crops that can be easily mowed or crimped are preferred in such systems.

7. Integration with Livestock

Cover crops can offer dual benefits when integrated with livestock farming:

- **Forage Value:** Some cover crops, like triticale and clover, provide excellent forage for livestock. This integration creates a multifunctional agricultural system where the cover crop benefits the soil and provides feed for animals.

In summary, the selection of cover crops is a multifaceted decision that requires careful consideration of agricultural goals, soil types, climate conditions, pest and disease management, economic factors, and potential integration with livestock. By meticulously selecting the appropriate cover crops, farmers can significantly enhance soil health, improve crop yields, and contribute to sustainable agricultural practices.

Composting Techniques

Overview of Composting

Composting is a natural process of recycling organic matter, such as leaves, vegetable scraps, and manure, into a valuable soil amendment known as compost. It's a cornerstone of organic farming and gardening, transforming waste into a resource that enriches soil, reduces the need for chemical fertilizers, and helps combat climate change by sequestering carbon.

Types of Composting Techniques

1. **Hot Composting** — Hot composting, also known as active composting, involves managing compost to reach higher temperatures (between 130°F and 160°F). These temperatures are achieved by balancing carbon-rich "brown" materials (like dried leaves) and nitrogen-rich "green" materials (like kitchen scraps), maintaining adequate moisture, and frequent turning. The high temperatures kill pathogens and weed seeds and accelerate decomposition. A study from Cornell University suggests that properly managed hot compost piles can break down organic material in as little as 18 days.
2. **Cold Composting** — Cold composting is a less intensive method. It involves simply piling up garden waste, kitchen scraps, and other organic materials and leaving them to decompose over time. This method is

less labor-intensive but takes longer (6 months to 2 years) and may not generate enough heat to kill weed seeds and pathogens.
3. **Vermicomposting** — Vermicomposting uses earthworms to break down organic matter. It's particularly effective for processing kitchen scraps. The worms consume organic waste and produce worm castings, a highly nutrient-rich compost. According to the University of California, vermicomposting can be done indoors or outdoors, making it versatile for different scales of operation.
4. **Bokashi Fermentation** — Bokashi is a Japanese method that ferments organic waste, including meat and dairy, which is typically not recommended for other composting methods. It involves layering waste with Bokashi bran in a sealed container and allowing it to ferment. The process is odor-free and fast, usually taking about two weeks. The fermented matter can then be buried in garden soil or added to traditional compost piles for further decomposition.

DIY Composting: Seven Steps

1. **Materials Collection** — Successful composting starts with collecting the right balance of materials. Your compost should have a mix of greens (kitchen scraps, fresh plant material) and browns (dry leaves, straw, or newspaper). The EPA estimates that about 28 percent of what we throw away could be composted.
2. **Layering** — Layering is key in composting. Start with a layer of browns, then add a layer of greens, and

repeat. This helps balance carbon and nitrogen in the pile and speeds up the decomposition process.
3. **Moisture and Aeration** — Moisture is critical — your compost pile should be as wet as a wrung-out sponge. Aeration is equally important for maintaining aerobic conditions. Turning the pile regularly introduces oxygen, which is essential for composting microorganisms. Without proper aeration, the composting process can become anaerobic, which is slower and can produce foul odors.
4. **Temperature Management** — In hot composting, temperature is an important indicator of the composting process. Ideally, the pile should reach 130°F to 160°F. At these temperatures, the composting is efficient, and harmful pathogens and weed seeds are destroyed. A compost thermometer can be used to monitor this.
5. **Turning and Mixing** — Regular turning (about once a week) is crucial for hot composting. It redistributes matter, ensuring even decomposition and maintaining oxygen levels. According to the University of Illinois Extension, turning compost can speed up the process by 50% or more.
6. **Maturation** — After the active composting phase, the compost should be left to mature. During this phase, which can last from a few months to a year, the compost continues to decompose at a slower rate and stabilizes. Mature compost is dark, crumbly, and has an earthy smell.
7. **Utilization of Compost** — Mature compost can be used as a soil amendment, mulch, or potting soil. It

improves soil structure, provides nutrients, enhances moisture retention, and can even suppress plant diseases. Research from the University of California Cooperative Extension shows that compost application can increase crop yields and improve soil health.

Preparing Quality Compost

1. **Ingredient Selection** — The quality of compost largely depends on the ingredients used. Avoid adding diseased plants, persistent weeds, or materials treated with pesticides. Including a variety of ingredients ensures a good balance of nutrients.
2. **Process Optimization** — Optimizing the composting process involves maintaining the right balance between greens and browns, ensuring adequate moisture and aeration, and managing the pile's temperature. This balance is key to efficient decomposition and high-quality compost.
3. **Ensuring Nutrient Richness** — To ensure the nutrient richness of the compost, it's essential to incorporate a diverse range of organic materials. This diversity not only balances the carbon-to-nitrogen ratio, which is crucial for microbial activity but also results in a more comprehensive nutrient profile in the finished compost. For example, adding fruit and vegetable scraps can introduce potassium and phosphorus, while eggshells can add calcium.

   A study by the University of California Cooperative Extension found that a well-balanced compost can significantly improve soil nutrient levels, leading to healthier plant growth and reduced need for synthetic fertilizers. Additionally, regularly testing the compost for nutrient content and pH can help in adjusting the inputs for optimal results.

4. **Managing pH Levels** — The pH level of compost is another vital aspect. A neutral to slightly acidic pH is generally desired. Materials like coffee grounds and pine needles tend to lower the pH, making the compost more acidic, while eggshells and wood ash can raise the pH. Monitoring and adjusting the pH can make the compost suitable for a wider range of plants.

5. **Incorporating Biochar** — Recent advancements in composting include the addition of biochar, a form of charcoal produced from biomass. Biochar in compost has been shown to improve soil water retention, nutrient retention, and microbial activity. A study published in the journal "Soil Biology and Biochemistry" found that biochar-compost blends can significantly enhance soil fertility and carbon sequestration.

6. **Preventing Contaminants** — Being cautious about what goes into the compost pile is crucial to prevent contaminants. Avoid adding meats, oils, and dairy products in traditional composting methods, as they can attract pests and produce odors. In addition, being mindful of plant material treated with pesticides or herbicides is important to keep the compost safe for use in gardens.

7. **Maturity Indicators** — Determining when compost is mature is crucial. Mature compost should be dark, crumbly, and have an earthy smell, with no

recognizable food or yard waste. Immature compost can harm plants due to the ongoing microbial activity, which can compete with plants for nutrients. The use of a compost maturity test kit can be beneficial in large-scale or commercial composting operations.

Troubleshooting Common Composting Issues

1. **Odor Problems** — Bad odors are usually a sign of anaerobic decomposition. This can be resolved by turning the compost to introduce oxygen, adding more brown materials to balance moisture, or decreasing the size of the compost pile.
2. **Pest Attraction** — To avoid attracting pests like rodents and flies, keep meat, dairy, and oily foods out of the compost, use a compost bin with a lid, and bury food scraps deep within the compost pile.
3. **Slow Decomposition** — If the composting process is unusually slow, it might be due to a lack of nitrogen, moisture, or poor aeration. Adding more green materials, ensuring adequate moisture, and turning the pile more frequently can help speed up the process.
4. **Temperature Fluctuations** — Fluctuating temperatures in a hot compost pile can indicate uneven moisture levels, insufficient aeration, or a lack of nitrogen-rich materials. Regular turning and monitoring can help maintain consistent temperatures.

Natural Fertilizer Application

Understanding Natural Fertilizers

1. **Definition and Types** — Natural fertilizers, also known as organic fertilizers, are derived from animal or plant matter and include compost, manure, bone meal, and seaweed extracts. These fertilizers release nutrients slowly into the soil, improving soil structure, enhancing microbial life, and providing a sustainable nutrient source for plants. They come in various forms, including solids, liquids, and pellets.
2. **Comparison with Processed Fertilizers** — Unlike synthetic fertilizers, which are manufactured chemically and offer high nutrient content in an immediately available form, natural fertilizers release nutrients more slowly. This gradual release helps prevent nutrient runoff and buildup, reducing the risk of harming water sources. A study by the Rodale Institute showed that organic fertilizers can also improve soil health over the long term compared to synthetic alternatives.

Best Natural Fertilizers

1. Criteria for Selection

The selection of a natural fertilizer depends on specific crop needs, soil conditions, and environmental considerations. Factors include nutrient content, rate of nutrient release, ease of application, and cost-effectiveness.

2. Top Natural Fertilizers for Various Crops

- **Compost:** A balanced, all-purpose fertilizer suitable for most crops.

- **Manure:** High in nitrogen, best for crops requiring rich soil, like leafy vegetables.
- **Bone meal:** High in phosphorus, excellent for root crops and flowering plants.
- **Fish emulsion:** A liquid fertilizer that is good for quick nutrient boosts during the growing season.

Application Methods

1. Timing and Frequency

The application of natural fertilizers depends on the crop's growth stage and nutrient requirements. Typically, applying before or during planting and supplementing during the growing season is recommended. Over-application can be avoided by regularly testing soil nutrient levels.

2. Application Techniques for Different Crops

- **Broadcasting:** Spreading fertilizer evenly over the soil surface, used for larger fields.
- **Side dressing:** Applying fertilizer alongside rows of crops is beneficial for plants needing extra nutrients during growth.
- **Foliar sprays:** Applying liquid fertilizers directly to plant leaves, used for quick nutrient absorption.

3. Soil Type Considerations

Sandy soils, which drain quickly, may require more frequent fertilizer applications. In contrast, clay soils, which retain nutrients longer, may need less frequent but more thorough applications.

Case Studies and Examples

1. Successful Implementations

- An organic farm in Vermont successfully transitioned from synthetic to natural fertilizers, observing improved soil health and increased yields over several years.
- A study in California demonstrated that compost applications in vineyards improved grape yield and quality compared to synthetic fertilizer usage.

2. Comparative Analysis with Chemical Fertilizers

Research often shows that while chemical fertilizers can boost yields in the short term, long-term use can degrade soil health. In contrast, natural fertilizers build soil structure and fertility over time. For instance, a long-term study by the University of Nebraska found that fields treated with organic fertilizers had higher soil organic matter and better water retention than those treated with synthetic fertilizers.

Chapter Three — Building Soil Fertility (Part II)

Crop Rotation

The concept of crop rotation can be traced back thousands of years. Ancient civilizations, from the Romans to the Chinese, were aware of the importance of changing the crops they grew in their fields over time. They might not have understood the scientific nuances as we do today, but their observational wisdom led them to realize that rotating crops helped their fields stay productive.

In medieval Europe, a system known as the three-field system was widely practiced. Farmers would divide their land into three parts: one for autumn-sown crops, one for spring-sown crops, and one left fallow. This rotation not only maintained soil fertility but also provided a varied diet for the community.

What is Crop Rotation?

Fast forward to the present, and crop rotation has evolved into a scientifically backed agricultural practice. At its core, it involves alternating the types of crops grown on a piece of land through successive seasons or years. This rotation can be as simple as alternating between two crops, or it can involve a complex schedule of many different crops over several years.

The idea is to use the natural characteristics and requirements of various crops to the advantage of the soil and subsequent crops. For example, planting nitrogen-fixing legumes like peas or beans can enrich the soil, benefiting the next crop that might be more nitrogen-demanding.

The beauty of crop rotation lies in its simplicity and effectiveness. A practice honed over millennia, it stands today as a testament to the wisdom of combining traditional agricultural practices with modern scientific understanding. As we delve deeper into its benefits and applications, it's clear that crop rotation is not just about growing crops; it's about nurturing the land and preserving it for future generations.

Advantages of Crop Rotation

As we turn the pages of agricultural wisdom, we find crop rotation shining brightly as a beacon of sustainable farming. This chapter peels back the layers of this age-old practice, revealing how it not only nurtures the land but also secures a prosperous future for farmers and gardeners alike.

> 1. **Enhancing Soil Fertility through Nutrient Cycling**
> — At the heart of crop rotation is the concept of

nutrient cycling. Simply put, different crops have different appetites and offerings when it comes to soil nutrients. Legumes, such as beans and peas, are like nature's fertilizer factories. They have a unique ability to 'fix' nitrogen from the air and store it in their root nodules, enriching the soil. When you rotate these with nitrogen-loving crops like corn or wheat, the latter thrive on the nitrogen left behind, reducing the need for synthetic fertilizers.

Furthermore, varying crops also means varying root structures and decomposition rates, which contributes to better soil structure and organic matter content. Organic matter is crucial – it's like a sponge that holds water and nutrients, making them readily available to plants. This enhances the overall health and fertility of the soil, creating a strong foundation for healthy crops.

2. **Managing Pests and Diseases** — Crop rotation is a **natural** sentinel against the relentless march of pests and diseases. Many of these undesirables are crop-specific; they set up camp in soil or plant residues, waiting for the next season of their favorite host. By rotating crops, you essentially pull the rug from under their feet. Without their preferred environment, their populations dwindle, significantly reducing the risk of outbreaks.

It's not just about what the crops put into the soil; it's also about what they don't take out. Different plants have different nutritional needs and pest vulnerabilities. By switching up your crops, you prevent the depletion of specific nutrients and reduce the buildup of pests and diseases associated with a particular plant. This means less reliance on chemical fertilizers and pesticides, leading to cost savings and a healthier, more sustainable environment.

Take, for instance, the classic battle against the infamous potato blight. Follow potatoes with a non-host crop like corn, and you'll break the life cycle of the blight, keeping it in check.

3. **Weed Warfare with Crop Rotation** — Weeds, the uninvited guests of the farming world, can be effectively managed with crop rotation. Different crops compete differently with weeds. Some, like rye, are allelopathic — they release chemicals that inhibit weed growth. Others have dense foliage or rapid growth, which shades the ground, making it hard for weeds to establish.

This natural method of weed control reduces your reliance on herbicides, leading to a healthier ecosystem and saving costs.

4. **Boosting Crop Yield and Quality** — Diverse is robust — this saying holds true in crop rotation. When crops are rotated, they grow healthier and more vigorously. This vigor translates into higher yields and better-quality produce. Think of it as a rest and recovery phase for the soil; each new crop benefits from the recuperation period afforded by its predecessor.

Studies have shown that crop rotation can lead to yield increases of up to 10-25%. That's not just more food; it's more nutritious, flavorful food, with studies indicating higher vitamin and mineral contents in rotationally grown crops.

5. **Pillar of Environmental Sustainability** — Crop rotation is a silent hero in the quest for environmental sustainability. By enhancing soil health, it plays a critical role in carbon sequestration — the process of capturing and storing atmospheric carbon dioxide. Healthy soils rich in organic matter can store vast amounts of carbon, helping to mitigate climate change.

   Moreover, rotation promotes biodiversity both above and below the soil surface. It creates varied habitats for a multitude of organisms, from beneficial insects to microorganisms, each playing a crucial role in the ecological balance.

6. **Enhancement of Biodiversity Within the Farm Ecosystem** — Diversity is nature's insurance policy. Each crop you plant supports a variety of insects, birds, and other organisms. This variety creates a more balanced ecosystem, where pest populations are naturally controlled by their predators, reducing the need for pesticides. Plus, a diverse ecosystem is more resilient to disease, extreme weather, and other environmental stresses.

Disadvantages of Crop Rotation

1. **Complexity and Need for Careful Planning and Knowledge** — Planning a successful crop rotation isn't just about randomly choosing different crops. It

requires an understanding of what each crop needs and what it leaves behind. You need to know the growing seasons, nutrient requirements, and pest and disease risks for each plant. This can be daunting, especially for beginners. However, with a bit of research and perhaps some advice from experienced farmers or local agricultural extension services, you can devise a plan that works for your land.

2. **Initial Costs and Labor Involved in Implementing Crop Rotation** — Switching to crop rotation can involve some upfront costs. You might need to invest in new seeds or plants, and the learning curve can mean some trial and error, which can be costly. Additionally, preparing your land for different types of crops each season can require more labor than sticking with a single crop. However, these initial investments often pay off in the long term with healthier soil, higher yields, and reduced need for expensive chemicals.

3. **Limitations Based on Specific Soil Types and Climatic Conditions** — Not all crops are suitable for all types of soil or climates. Some plants might thrive in your neighbor's field but struggle in yours due to slight differences in soil composition or microclimate. It's important to choose crops that are well-suited to your specific conditions. This might limit the variety of crops you can rotate, but with careful selection, you can still reap many of the benefits of crop rotation.

Management Requirements in Crop Rotation

In the world of small-scale farming and home gardening, a successful yield often hinges on the wise management of your resources and knowledge. One key aspect of this is understanding and implementing effective crop rotation. Let's break down what this means and how you can use it to benefit your land.

- **Strategic Crop Selection and Sequencing** — Firstly, knowing your soil type is like knowing the personality of your best friend – it helps you make the best decisions. Soil types can vary greatly, from sandy to clay-heavy, and each type has its own needs and characteristics. For instance, sandy soil drains quickly but may not hold nutrients well, while clay soil retains moisture but might have poor drainage.

  Here's where strategic crop selection comes in. Different crops have different nutrient needs and impacts on the soil. For example, legumes like beans and peas are known as 'nitrogen fixers' – they help to add nitrogen back into the soil. So, planting these before a crop that needs a lot of nitrogen, like corn, is a smart move. This is an example of sequencing: choosing the order of crops in a way that benefits the soil and subsequent crops.
- **The Importance of Soil Testing and Analysis** — To make informed decisions, you need information. Soil testing is like getting a health check-up for your soil. It tells you about its nutrient levels, pH

balance, and other important factors. This information is crucial for two reasons:
- **Nutrient Management:** You'll know what your soil is lacking and can add fertilizers accordingly. Too much of any nutrient can be just as harmful as too little.
- **Tailored Crop Selection:** Understanding your soil's condition helps you choose crops that will grow well in it, leading to better yields.

Local agricultural extension offices often offer soil testing services or can guide you on how to do it yourself.

- **Adjusting Timing and Rotation Patterns** — Crop rotation isn't just about what you plant; it's also about when and how often. The goal is to avoid planting the same type of crop in the same place too often. This practice reduces the risk of soil nutrient depletion and the buildup of pests and diseases associated with a particular crop.

  The rotation pattern depends on the crops you're growing. For instance, a simple three-year rotation might involve planting a leafy crop (like lettuce), followed by a fruiting crop (like tomatoes), and then a root crop (like carrots). Adjust these patterns based on your observations and crop performance.

- **Adaptability in Response to Weather and Climate Change** — Lastly, remember that farming and gardening are at the mercy of the weather, which can be unpredictable. With the ongoing impacts of climate change, adaptability is key. This might mean altering your crop rotation schedule in response to unexpected weather patterns, like a sudden drought or extended rainy season.

For instance, if you're experiencing a particularly wet season, it might be wise to plant crops that can tolerate excess moisture or delay planting certain crops until conditions are more favorable.

Staying informed about local climate trends and forecasts can aid in this adaptability. Connect with local farmer groups or agricultural advisors who can provide insights and advice tailored to your region.

Diversified Planting

Diversified planting is like painting a canvas with a variety of crops instead of just one color. It's an approach that imitates the diversity found in nature, leading to a healthier, more resilient farm or garden. This section explores how to bring this concept to life in your fields.

Understanding Structural Diversity in Crop Systems

1. **Vertical Diversity:** Think of vertical diversity as stacking plants of different heights in the same area, like a forest, where tall trees canopy over shrubs and groundcovers. In your garden, this could mean planting tall corn alongside medium-height beans and low-growing squash. This maximizes space and can improve light and moisture utilization.
2. **Horizontal Diversity:** This involves spreading a variety of crops across your land horizontally. It's like a patchwork quilt, where each patch is a

different crop. By doing so, you reduce the risk of pest outbreaks, as pests that prefer one crop won't easily jump to another.
3. **Temporal Diversity:** This is all about timing. Different crops mature at different times, so planting a mix can give you a steady harvest throughout the season. For example, radishes mature quickly, while carrots take longer. Planting both gives you an early crop of radishes and a later crop of carrots.

Strategies to Increase Crop Diversity

- **Polycultures:** This means growing multiple crop species together. It's like a mini-ecosystem in your field. Polycultures can lead to better soil health and reduced pest problems. For example, planting marigolds among your vegetables can deter certain pests naturally.
- **Multi cropping:** This is the practice of growing more than one type of crop in the same space over a growing season. For instance, after harvesting early-season lettuce, you might plant a late-season crop like broccoli in the same space.
- **Intercropping:** Here, you grow two or more crops close together. The idea is that the different crops will benefit each other. For instance, planting nitrogen-fixing peas alongside nitrogen-hungry corn can improve overall soil fertility.
- **Cover Crops and Green Manures:** Cover crops, like clover or rye, are planted not to be harvested but to cover the soil, prevent erosion, and improve

soil health. When these are turned into the soil, they act as green manures, adding organic matter and nutrients. This is an excellent way to prepare your field for the next growing season.

Implementing These Strategies

Start small and experiment. You might try a few tomato plants with basil and marigolds around them. Observe how they grow together. Use local knowledge and resources – neighboring farmers or gardening groups can be invaluable. Remember, diversified planting not only benefits your crops but also contributes to a healthier ecosystem and, ultimately, a more sustainable form of agriculture.

Popular Farm Diversification Strategies

As a seasoned farmer with years of hands-on experience, I've learned that success in agriculture often means thinking outside the traditional crop box. Diversification, or the practice of expanding the range of products and services offered on a farm, is crucial for resilience and profitability. In this chapter, I'll delve into some of the most effective diversification strategies that have been gaining popularity among small-scale farmers and home gardeners. We'll explore agrotourism and educational programs, the shift toward organic and specialty crops, and the integration of livestock and aquaculture.

Agrotourism and Educational Programs

Agrotourism, sometimes referred to as agritourism, is a fantastic way for farms to open their gates to the public for recreational and educational purposes. This trend is not just about giving city dwellers a taste of country life; it's about creating immersive experiences that connect people to the source of their food. From pick-your-own fruit ventures and farm stays to guided tours and workshops on sustainable farming practices, agrotourism provides a multifaceted income stream.

For example, a small orchard might offer apple-picking experiences in the fall, complete with hayrides and cider-tasting. These activities not only generate additional revenue but also educate the public about local agriculture. Educational programs can range from school field trips to hands-on workshops on topics like beekeeping or organic gardening.

The beauty of agrotourism lies in its dual purpose: it promotes agriculture while simultaneously providing entertainment and education. This engagement is especially important in a world where many are disconnected from the origins of their food.

Shift Toward Organic and Specialty Crop Production

In recent years, there's been a significant shift toward organic and specialty crop production. This move is driven by increasing consumer demand for healthier, environmentally friendly food options. Organic farming, which avoids synthetic fertilizers and pesticides, can be more labor-intensive, but it often commands higher market prices.

Specialty crops, like heirloom vegetables, exotic fruits, or medicinal herbs, offer unique opportunities. These crops are often not widely available in larger commercial markets, giving small-scale farmers a niche to explore. For instance, growing heirloom tomatoes or rare chili pepper varieties can attract customers who are looking for something different than what's available in their local supermarket.

Diversifying into organic and specialty crops is not just about tapping into a market trend; it's also about sustainability. These practices promote biodiversity, improve soil health, and reduce our carbon footprint, contributing to a healthier planet.

Integration of Livestock and Aquaculture

Another diversification strategy is integrating livestock and aquaculture into farming operations. This approach creates a more dynamic agricultural system, where different parts of the farm work together in synergy. For instance, chickens can be raised not only for their eggs and meat but also to control pests and fertilize crops. Similarly, integrating aquaculture, such as fish farming, can complement plant-growing systems, especially in aquaponics setups where fish waste provides nutrients for plants.

This integrated approach helps recycle and efficiently use resources on the farm. It also spreads the financial risk; if one aspect of the farm underperforms, others can compensate. For example, a farm experiencing a poor vegetable harvest can still rely on income from dairy production or fish sales.

By embracing these diversification strategies, farmers and gardeners can not only enhance their income but also contribute to a more sustainable and environmentally responsible agricultural system. These methods, while requiring effort and adaptation, offer a pathway to a resilient and rewarding farming future.

Approachable Strategies for Sustainable Farming

Farming is not just about growing crops or raising livestock; it's about nurturing the earth and our communities. As a farmer with years of experience in the field, I've witnessed firsthand the transformative power of sustainable practices. In this chapter, we will explore several approachable strategies that can make a big difference, whether you're running a small family farm or managing a home garden.

Conversion to Organic Farming

Organic farming is a method that emphasizes the use of natural processes and materials, shunning synthetic fertilizers, pesticides, and genetically modified organisms (GMOs). It's not just a farming style — it's a commitment to working harmoniously with nature. But how does one transition from conventional to organic farming?

1. **Soil Health:** Start with the soil. Organic farming relies on healthy, living soil rich in organic matter. Composting, crop rotations, and using green manures are excellent ways to enrich your soil.
2. **Pest Management:** Instead of synthetic pesticides, organic farmers use biological pest control. This could mean introducing beneficial insects that prey on harmful pests or using natural plant extracts.
3. **Weed Control:** Forget about chemical herbicides. Organic farmers often use mulching, manual weeding, and cover crops to manage weeds.

The benefits? Healthier soil, more nutritious crops, and a safer environment for our families and wildlife. Remember, the transition to organic farming doesn't happen overnight—it's a gradual process of learning and adapting.

Low-Till and No-Till Farming Practices

Tillage is the agricultural practice of preparing the soil for planting by turning it over. However, excessive tillage can lead to soil erosion, loss of organic matter, and disruption of soil ecosystems. This is where low-till and no-till methods come in:

- **Low-Till Farming:** This involves minimal disturbance of the soil. Tools like chisel plows that don't turn the soil over are used instead.
- **No-Till Farming:** As the name suggests, no-till farming means not tilling the soil at all. Seeds are directly planted into the residue of previous crops.

The benefits are significant: reduced soil erosion, improved water retention, and enhanced soil health. Not to mention, it's a time and fuel saver!

Utilization of Renewable Energy Sources

Farming requires energy, and renewable sources like solar, wind, and bioenergy are game-changers. Solar panels can power farm operations, while wind turbines can harness the power of the wind. Bioenergy, derived from agricultural waste, can be another valuable energy source.

Using renewable energy reduces dependency on non-renewable resources, cuts down on greenhouse gas emissions, and can even be a source of additional income (think selling excess energy back to the grid).

Community Supported Agriculture (CSA) Programs

CSAs are a bridge between farmers and consumers. In a CSA, consumers buy "shares" of a farm's harvest in advance, and in return, they receive regular allotments of fresh produce throughout the farming season.

The benefits? For farmers, it provides a direct market for their produce and upfront capital. For consumers, it's a way to get fresh, local produce and connect with where their food comes from.

Companion Planting for Maximum Yield

In the heart of every flourishing garden, there's an unspoken camaraderie, a relationship that thrives beneath the soil and amongst the greenery. This is the essence of companion planting, a method that has been embraced by farmers and gardeners alike for centuries. As an experienced cultivator, I've seen firsthand the wonders of this approach and aim to share its nuances, particularly to aid small-scale farmers and home gardeners in achieving a bountiful harvest.

What is Companion Planting?

At its core, companion planting is the strategic placement of different crops in close proximity for pest control and pollination, providing habitat for beneficial insects, maximizing the use of space, and increasing crop productivity. This method embraces the concept that certain plants can benefit each other when grown together.

The benefits of companion planting are numerous. For instance, some plants can repel pests naturally, reducing the need for chemical pesticides. Others can improve soil health, provide shade, or support the growth of their neighbors.

Understanding the Companion Planting Chart

A companion planting chart is an essential tool for gardeners. It provides a clear guide on which plants are companions (beneficial to each other) and which are foes (detrimental to each other). For instance, tomatoes thrive when planted alongside basil and onions, but they should not be planted near cabbages. Understanding these pairings is crucial in planning your garden layout.

Effective Companion Planting Pairs

Let's explore some of the most successful companion planting pairs:

1. **Tomatoes and Basil:** This classic pair benefits from basil's ability to repel flies and mosquitoes while also reportedly improving the flavor of tomatoes. It's a perfect example of how companion planting caters to both pest control and flavor enhancement.
2. **Carrots and Onions:** Onions can repel the carrot fly, a common pest for carrots, making them a

practical pairing for maximizing yield and minimizing crop damage.
3. **Cucumbers and Nasturtiums:** Nasturtiums are not only beautiful, but they also serve as a trap crop for pests that would otherwise target cucumbers.
4. **Beans and Corn:** Beans can fix nitrogen in the soil, providing nutrients for corn, while cornstalks offer a natural trellis for beans to climb.
5. **Lettuce and Tall Flowers:** Tall flowers can provide shade for lettuce, which thrives in cooler temperatures, thereby extending its growing season.

Avoiding Incompatible Pairings

Just as some plants benefit each other, others can be detrimental when placed together. For instance:

- Tomatoes should not be planted near potatoes as they share common diseases, which can spread more easily if they are close.
- Beans and onions are a bad combination as onions can inhibit the growth of beans.

Implementing Companion Planting in Your Garden

Here are some tips for implementing companion planting in your garden:

1. **Start with a Plan:** Assess your garden space and create a layout based on the companion planting chart. Consider factors like sunlight, soil type, and water requirements.

2. **Rotate Crops Annually:** This prevents soil depletion and reduces disease and pest buildup. For example, follow nitrogen-fixing beans with nitrogen-loving corn.
3. **Incorporate Flowers and Herbs:** These can attract beneficial insects and repel pests. For instance, marigolds are known to deter nematodes and other garden pests.
4. **Observe and Adapt:** Monitor your garden's progress and adapt as needed. What works in one area or season may not work in another.

Real-World Examples of Companion Planting

Three Sisters Farming (Native American Agriculture):

- **Background:** One of the most famous examples of companion planting is the "Three Sisters" method used by various Native American tribes. This technique involves planting corn, beans, and squash together.
- **Implementation:** The corn provides a structure for the beans to climb, the beans fix nitrogen in the soil, benefiting the other two plants, and the squash spreads along the ground, blocking the sunlight, which helps prevent weeds.
- **Outcome:** The combination of these three plants results in a mutually beneficial relationship, improving soil fertility and yielding a balanced diet from a single plot of land.

Rice-Fish Co-Culture in Asian Agriculture:

- **Background:** Practiced for over 1,200 years in parts of Asia, this method involves growing rice and raising fish simultaneously in the same field.
- **Implementation:** The fish contribute to the ecosystem by eating pests and weeds and fertilizing the rice paddies with their waste.
- **Outcome:** This method increases rice yields, provides a protein source from the fish, and reduces the need for chemical pesticides and fertilizers.

Apple Orchards and Companion Planting in Europe:

- **Background:** Many European apple orchards utilize companion planting to enhance biodiversity and control pests.
- **Implementation:** Flowers like daisies and clovers are planted between apple trees. These flowers attract pollinators and beneficial insects that prey on apple pests.
- **Outcome:** This approach has been found to reduce pest populations, decrease the need for chemical pesticides, and increase apple yields.

Marigold and Tomato Pairing in Home Gardens:

- **Background:** Gardeners often plant marigolds alongside tomatoes.
- **Implementation:** Marigolds are known to repel nematodes, whiteflies, and even rabbits. Their strong scent is believed to mask the smell of the tomatoes, making them less attractive to pests.

- **Outcome:** Gardeners report healthier tomato plants with fewer pest problems. Some also believe marigolds improve the flavor of tomatoes.

Intercropping in Sub-Saharan Africa:

- **Background:** In many African countries, farmers practice intercropping to maximize limited land resources.
- **Implementation:** Crops like maize are intercropped with legumes such as beans and peas.
- **Outcome:** The legumes fix nitrogen in the soil, which benefits the maize. This practice leads to better soil health, higher yields, and improved food security.

Hop and Hemp Synergy in North America:

- **Background:** Some North American farmers have experimented with planting hops and hemp together.
- **Implementation:** Both crops benefit from similar growing conditions, and the diversity helps manage pests and diseases that could otherwise devastate a monoculture crop.
- **Outcome:** Preliminary reports suggest increased yield and quality in both crops, with a natural reduction in pest populations.

As we turn the final page of this chapter on "Building Soil Health," it is essential to reflect on the profound insights and sustainable strategies presented, which are pivotal for the well-being of our soil and, by extension, the health of our ecosystems and communities.

Soil, the foundation of our agricultural world, is more than just a medium for growing crops; it's a vibrant ecosystem teeming with life. Through this chapter, we delved into the intricacies of soil fertility, understanding that it's not just about the presence of essential nutrients but also about the complex interplay of biological, chemical, and physical factors. This holistic view is crucial for appreciating the true value of healthy soil.

Chapter Four — Water Management

As someone who has spent years with my hands in the soil, nurturing crops from seed to harvest, I understand the vital role that water plays in agriculture. Whether you're managing acres of farmland or nurturing a backyard garden, effective water management is key to your success. In this chapter, we'll delve into the intricacies of water management, aiming to provide you with practical insights and actionable advice.

Water, as we all know, is a lifeline for plants. It's not just about quenching their thirst; water is essential for the physiological processes of a plant, like photosynthesis, where plants convert sunlight into energy. But here's the catch: too little water and your crops can wither and die; too much and you might drown them or encourage diseases. So, how do we strike the perfect balance? This is where efficient water management comes into play.

Think of water management as a balancing act. It's about ensuring that your plants receive the right amount of water at the right time. This might sound simple, but it involves a deep understanding of your plant's needs, the soil type, local weather patterns, and available water resources. For small-scale farmers and home gardeners, mastering this balance can mean the difference between a bountiful harvest and a disappointing yield.

One of the most important concepts in water management is irrigation efficiency. This refers to how well water is delivered to your plants without wastage. Imagine you're watering your garden with a hose, but half of the water is landing on the sidewalk or evaporating into thin air. That's low efficiency. High efficiency is when most of the water you apply is used by the plants. We'll explore various irrigation techniques, from simple methods like rainwater harvesting to sophisticated drip irrigation systems, and provide tips on how to choose and optimize them for your specific needs.

As we journey through this chapter, remember that every drop of water counts. In many parts of the world, water is a scarce resource, and its wise use is not just beneficial for our crops but also for the environment. Let's explore together how we can become stewards of this precious resource, ensuring healthy crops and a sustainable future for our farming and gardening endeavors.

Efficient Irrigation Practices

In the realm of agriculture, irrigation is more than just watering plants; it's a critical lifeline. The essence of irrigation lies in artificially supplying water to land or soil to assist in the growth of crops. This technique is particularly vital in regions where rainfall is insufficient or erratic. From my experience, irrigation can boost crop yield, enhance soil quality, and even extend the growing season in colder climates. It's not merely about providing water; it's about creating an optimal environment for crops to flourish.

Tracing back to ancient civilizations, irrigation has been a cornerstone of agriculture. The Egyptians harnessed the Nile's floods, and the Mesopotamians engineered intricate canal systems. These early innovations reveal a profound understanding of water management that has evolved over centuries. Today, we stand on the shoulders of these agricultural giants, integrating traditional wisdom with modern technology to cultivate our crops.

Best Irrigation Techniques

Surface Irrigation

Surface irrigation, one of the oldest methods, involves distributing water over the soil surface, primarily driven by gravity. It's akin to the way rainwater spreads across a field. This method can be broken down into further sub-types, such as furrow, flood, or basin irrigation. The key to success with surface irrigation lies in understanding the landscape and soil. For instance, in my own experience, leveling the field can significantly improve the distribution of water and reduce wastage. However, it's important to note that this method can be less efficient in terms of water usage, as evaporation and runoff are common issues.

Drip Irrigation

Drip irrigation, a method I highly recommend, involves delivering water directly to the root zone of the plant through a network of pipes and emitters. This system minimizes water loss due to evaporation and runoff, making it one of the most water-efficient methods available. It's particularly effective in arid regions and for crops that require precise water management, like vegetables and fruit trees. The precision it offers allows for controlled watering, which can lead to increased crop yield and quality. Additionally, drip systems can be integrated with water-soluble fertilizers, optimizing plant nutrition.

Sprinkler Irrigation

Sprinkler systems simulate natural rainfall by distributing water through a system of pipes and spray heads. This method is versatile and suitable for various terrains and crop types. I've seen it work wonders in large fields and small gardens alike. The key advantages include its ability to cover large areas and its ease of installation and operation. However, it's crucial to consider factors like wind and evaporation, which can affect water distribution. Adjusting the timing of irrigation to early morning or late evening can mitigate these issues.

Subsurface Irrigation

Subsurface irrigation is a technologically advanced method where water is supplied directly to the root zone beneath the soil surface. This system maximizes water efficiency by minimizing losses due to evaporation and surface runoff. It's particularly beneficial in sandy soils where surface irrigation might lead to quick drainage. Though its initial setup cost can be high, the long-term benefits in water savings and crop yield can be significant. As an expert farmer, I recommend this for high-value crops and in areas where water conservation is apriority.

Evaluating Irrigation Efficiency

Water-Use Efficiency Metrics

Water-use efficiency in irrigation can be quantified through various metrics. The most straightforward is the ratio of the amount of water beneficially used by the plants to the total amount of water applied. For instance, if 70% of the water applied is utilized by the crop, the efficiency is 70%. However, this simplistic metric doesn't always capture the complexity of agricultural water use. Factors like deep percolation, which can replenish groundwater, or runoff that can be reused downstream, should also be considered in broader efficiency evaluations.

Factors Influencing Efficiency

Numerous factors influence irrigation efficiency. The soil type is crucial; for example, loamy soils with good structure and water-holding capacity can make the most of each irrigation event. Another factor is the crop type; deep-rooted crops might utilize water more efficiently than shallow-rooted ones. Climate plays a significant role, too; in hot, windy conditions, evaporation rates can skyrocket, demanding more frequent irrigation. The design, installation, and maintenance of the irrigation system are also critical. A poorly maintained drip system with clogged emitters, for instance, can drastically reduce its efficiency.

Case Studies of Efficiency Rates

Worldwide, numerous success stories exemplify the benefits of efficient irrigation. These systems not only save water but also improve crop quality by providing consistent moisture directly to the plant roots. Another example can be seen in the rice terraces of the Philippines, a UNESCO World Heritage site. Here, ancient techniques of water management have sustained generations, showcasing a harmonious balance between human needs and ecological preservation. In the western United States, where water scarcity is a growing concern, precision irrigation techniques have been adopted to maximize the utility of limited water resources.

Enhancing Irrigation Efficiency for Farmers

Enhancing irrigation efficiency is akin to tuning a well-oiled machine; it requires precision, understanding, and a willingness to adapt. Through my years in farming, I've seen how small adjustments can yield significant improvements. In this section, we'll explore strategies for enhancing irrigation efficiency, address common challenges, and discuss practical solutions.

Strategies for Increasing Efficiency

Improved Irrigation Scheduling

Proper irrigation scheduling is vital. It's about watering crops at the right time and in the right amount, optimizing water use while maintaining crop health. The old method of watering on a fixed schedule, regardless of the crop's actual water needs, is inefficient. Today, scheduling should be based on various factors like the crop's growth stage, soil type, and local weather conditions.

Let's take the example of a technique I employ, known as 'deficit irrigation.' This involves deliberately applying less water than the crop requires, encouraging deeper root growth and enhancing drought resistance. However, precise knowledge of the crop's water needs and careful monitoring are required to avoid stress.

Adoption of Technology and Automation

Embracing technology in irrigation can be a game-changer. Automated irrigation systems can save time and improve water efficiency. Technologies like programmable timers, soil moisture sensors, and weather-based controllers can automate the irrigation process, ensuring that crops receive water only when needed.

For example, I've seen farmers use smart controllers that adjust watering schedules based on real-time weather data. This technology can reduce water use significantly, as it prevents unnecessary watering during rainy periods or adjusts for hotter conditions.

Soil Moisture Monitoring

Understanding soil moisture levels is crucial for efficient irrigation. Over-watering not only wastes water but can also harm crops, promote disease, and lead to nutrient leaching. Soil moisture sensors can provide real-time data, allowing farmers to irrigate only when necessary.

I've utilized tensiometers, which measure soil water tension, and capacitance sensors, which measure the volumetric water content. By integrating these tools into my irrigation practices, I've been able to significantly reduce water usage while maintaining crop health and yield.

Challenges and Solutions

Economic Barriers

One of the primary challenges in enhancing irrigation efficiency is the cost associated with adopting new technologies or changing existing systems. For many small-scale farmers, the initial investment can be prohibitive.

The solution here can be multifaceted. Government subsidies or grants can play a crucial role in easing financial burdens. Additionally, implementing cost-effective technologies, like simple soil moisture sensors, can be a step in the right direction. Even low-tech solutions, like rainwater harvesting or mulching to reduce evaporation, can be economical and effective.

Climate-Related Challenges

Climate variability presents a significant challenge to efficient irrigation. Droughts, unpredictable rainfall, and extreme temperatures can make water management increasingly difficult.

Diversifying irrigation methods can be a solution. For instance, combining rainwater harvesting with efficient irrigation techniques can provide a buffer during dry spells. Additionally, selecting drought-resistant crop varieties and practicing soil conservation techniques can mitigate the effects of climate variability.

Education and Training

A lack of knowledge and training can hinder the adoption of efficient irrigation practices. Many farmers are unaware of the latest technologies or techniques that can optimize water usage.

Here, education and community engagement are key. Conducting workshops, field demonstrations, and extension services can equip farmers with the necessary knowledge.

Collaborative efforts between agricultural institutes, local governments, and farming communities can foster a culture of learning and innovation.

Smart Irrigation Practices

In a world where the demand for agricultural efficiency and sustainability is at an all-time high, 'smart' irrigation practices are no longer a luxury but a necessity. This section will guide you through the concept of smart irrigation, its technological advancements, and real-world applications that can be adopted by both small-scale farmers and avid gardeners.

Definition and Relevance

Smart irrigation refers to the use of technology to optimize water usage in irrigation practices. It's about being *smart* with water — using the right amount at the right time for the right crop. The relevance of smart irrigation in today's world is paramount, particularly in the face of climate change and water scarcity. It offers a solution to water waste and helps in the production of healthy crops by providing precise water management.

Technological Innovations in Irrigation

Sensor-Based Systems

Sensor technology has revolutionized irrigation practices. Soil moisture sensors, for instance, are devices that measure the moisture content in the soil, enabling farmers to understand when the crops need water. This removes the guesswork and prevents both over and under-watering. There are various types of soil moisture sensors, like tensiometers and neutron moisture meters, each suitable for different soil types and conditions.

Furthermore, weather sensors can track parameters like rainfall, temperature, humidity, and wind speed, helping to adjust irrigation schedules based on current weather conditions. Integration of these sensors into an irrigation system ensures that plants receive the exact amount of water they need, maximizing efficiency.

Automated Irrigation Controls

Automation in irrigation involves using controllers to turn irrigation systems on and off at predetermined times. Advances in this technology have led to the development of smart controllers, which can automatically adjust watering schedules based on real-time data from weather and soil moisture sensors.

For example, a smart controller can reduce or skip watering cycles during rainy days or increase them during hot spells. This not only saves water but also ensures that crops are not stressed due to inconsistent watering. These systems can often be managed remotely via smartphones, offering convenience and control to the farmer.

Data-Driven Irrigation Management

This involves the analysis of data collected from various sources, like soil sensors, weather stations, and even satellite imagery, to make informed irrigation decisions. Data-driven irrigation management can help predict irrigation needs, track water usage, and even identify potential issues before they become problems.

By utilizing data analytics and machine learning algorithms, farmers can gain insights into patterns and trends in their irrigation practices, leading to more refined and efficient water management strategies.

Case Studies: Implementation and Results

California Almond Farms

In California, where water scarcity is a pressing issue, almond farmers have adopted smart irrigation practices to optimize water use. By using soil moisture sensors and weather data, they have been able to reduce water usage by up to 20% while maintaining or improving yield. This not only conserves water but also enhances the quality of the almonds.

Vineyards in France

Some vineyards in France have implemented sensor-based irrigation systems to maintain the perfect soil moisture level for grape cultivation. These systems provide precise watering that adapts to each vine's needs, significantly improving the quality of the wine while reducing water usage.

Rice Fields in Japan

In Japan, where rice is a staple crop, farmers have utilized automated irrigation systems coupled with weather forecasting data. This smart irrigation practice has enabled them to adjust water levels in their rice paddies, reducing water use and labor costs and resulting in a more sustainable and productive farming operation.

Watering Systems in Agriculture

Navigating through the myriad of watering systems available today can be like walking through a maze. In this section, I aim to shed light on the different types of watering systems used in agriculture, helping you understand their intricacies and how to select the best option for your specific needs.

Types of Watering Systems

Manual Watering Systems

The most basic form of irrigation, manual watering, is still widely used, especially in small gardens and farms. It typically involves using hoses, watering cans, or simple sprinklers that are operated by hand. The beauty of manual watering lies in its simplicity and direct control. You can see exactly where the water is going and how much is being applied.

One popular method of manual watering is the use of soaker hoses. These hoses are laid out along the rows of plants, slowly seeping water directly into the soil. This method is effective in reducing water waste and preventing the spread of leaf diseases caused by overhead watering.

Automated and Semi-Automated Systems

As we move up the technological ladder, we find automated and semi-automated systems. These include sprinkler systems, drip irrigation systems, and more advanced setups controlled by timers or smart systems.

Automated sprinkler systems are common in larger farming operations and landscapes, and they can cover large areas efficiently. They can be set to operate on a schedule, reducing the labor involved in manual systems.

Drip irrigation, as discussed earlier, can also be automated. The use of timers and controllers allows for precise water delivery based on the specific needs of the plants, ensuring that water is not wasted.

Selection Criteria for Watering Systems

Crop Requirements

Different crops have different watering needs. Root depth, growth stage, and the plant's overall water requirements play a critical role in selecting the right watering system. For example, deep-rooted plants might benefit more from drip irrigation systems that deliver water directly to the root zone. In contrast, shallow-rooted plants may do well with surface systems like sprinklers.

Additionally, the spacing of crops can influence the choice. Wide-spaced crops might be better served by individual emitters in a drip system, whereas closely planted crops might be more suited to soaker hoses or sprinklers.

Climate Considerations

The local climate is a crucial factor in selecting a watering system. In areas with high evaporation rates, like arid or hot climates, systems that minimize water loss (like drip irrigation) are preferable. In contrast, in regions with high humidity, where fungal diseases might be an issue, systems that avoid wetting the plant foliage, such as drip or soaker hoses, can be beneficial.

Wind is another factor. In windy areas, sprinkler systems might not be the best choice due to water drift and evaporation losses. In such scenarios, low-to-ground watering systems like drip lines are more effective.

Resource Availability

The availability of resources, including water, labor, and finances, also impacts the choice of watering system. For small-scale farmers or gardeners with limited water supplies, efficient systems like drip irrigation, which provide targeted watering and reduce waste, are ideal.

Labor availability is another consideration. In regions where labor is scarce or expensive, automated systems can be a blessing, saving time and labor costs. On the other hand, manual systems might be more feasible in areas where labor is readily available and less expensive.

Budget constraints play a significant role as well. While automated systems can be more cost-effective in the long run due to reduced water and labor costs, the initial investment might be higher compared to manual systems.

In conclusion, choosing the right watering system for agriculture is a complex decision that depends on a variety of factors. Understanding the specific needs of your crops, the local climate and your available resources is key to making an informed choice. Whether it's a simple manual system or a more advanced automated setup, the goal remains the same: to provide your plants with the water they need efficiently and sustainably. Remember, the right watering system not only promotes healthy plant growth but also conserves one of our most precious resources: water.

Role of Water in Crop Health

In agriculture, water is more than just a basic necessity for plant growth; it's the lifeblood of the entire ecosystem. In this section, we'll explore the multifaceted role of water in crop health, emphasizing its criticality, effects on various aspects of crop development, and real-world examples of effective water management.

Water as a Critical Resource

Water in agriculture serves multiple purposes beyond just quenching the plant's thirst. It's a solvent, a transporter, and a temperature regulator. It's involved in every physiological function of the plant, from germination through to maturity. The availability of water influences a plant's entire lifecycle, dictating not only if a plant will grow but also how well it grows.

Effects of Water Quality and Quantity on Crops

Growth and Yield

The quantity and timing of water supply directly influence the growth and yield of crops. Adequate water during critical growth stages, such as germination and flowering, is crucial for optimal development. In my experience, water-stressed plants often exhibit stunted growth and reduced yields. For instance, in grain crops like wheat, insufficient water during the grain-filling stage can lead to smaller, shriveled grains.

Disease Resistance

Water also plays a pivotal role in a plant's ability to resist diseases. Overhead irrigation methods can create wet foliage, which is conducive to the development of fungal diseases. On the other hand, a well-watered plant can better resist pests and diseases, as stress often makes plants more susceptible. Balanced moisture levels can help maintain robust plant structures and promote healthy foliage, lessening the likelihood of disease outbreaks.

Nutrient Uptake

Water is essential for the dissolution and transport of nutrients from the soil to the plant roots. Insufficient water limits a plant's ability to absorb essential nutrients, leading to deficiencies, even if the soil is rich in nutrients. Conversely, over-irrigation can leach away vital nutrients, reducing their availability to the plant. Therefore, precise water management is key to ensuring balanced nutrient uptake.

Case Studies: Impact of Water Management on Crop Health

California's Central Valley

In California's Central Valley, a region known for its agricultural productivity, water management has been a critical factor in maintaining crop health amid water scarcity. Farmers have adopted efficient irrigation practices like drip irrigation and deficit irrigation to optimize water use. These practices have not only conserved water but also resulted in healthier crops with improved yields. For example, tomato growers using drip irrigation have reported higher yields and better fruit quality compared to those using traditional flooding methods.

Rice Fields in India

In India, rice is a staple crop, traditionally grown in water-intensive flooded fields. However, innovative water management techniques like the System of Rice Intensification (SRI) have demonstrated that rice can be grown with less water yet produce higher yields. This method involves intermittent flooding and allows the soil to dry between irrigations, promoting better root development and plant health. Farmers practicing SRI have reported not only increased yields but also a significant reduction in water use and resistance to pest and disease outbreaks.

Apple Orchards in Washington State

Washington State, known for its apple production, has seen a transformation in water management practices. Orchards have shifted from high-volume overhead sprinklers to micro-irrigation systems, significantly improving water efficiency. This change has been crucial for apple health, as controlled water delivery has reduced the incidence of water-related diseases like apple scab and root rot while ensuring consistent fruit quality and size.

Rainwater Harvesting

Rainwater harvesting is a practice as ancient as agriculture itself, yet it remains a cornerstone of sustainable water management in modern times. This section delves into the concept, methods, challenges, global examples, and the sustainability of rainwater harvesting.

Introduction to Rainwater Harvesting

Definition and Principles

Rainwater harvesting is the practice of collecting, storing, and utilizing rainwater for agricultural, domestic, and environmental purposes. The principle behind it is simple yet profound: capture rainwater when it's available, store it, and use it during times of need. This method is particularly valuable in regions with distinct dry and wet seasons. It's not just about water conservation; it's also about maximizing the utility of a free and natural resource.

Historical and Cultural Context

Historically, rainwater harvesting has been a lifeline for civilizations in arid and semi-arid regions. Ancient structures like stepwells in India, underground cisterns in Rome, and the sophisticated water channels of the Incas in Peru are testimonies to early innovations in rainwater harvesting. These systems were not only practical solutions to water scarcity but also played a significant cultural and social role in these societies.

Methods of Rainwater Harvesting

Surface Runoff Harvesting

Surface runoff harvesting involves collecting rainwater from surfaces like fields, gardens, or open grounds. This method often includes building small check dams or ponds, which capture runoff water from higher ground. The stored water can then be used for irrigation, recharging groundwater, or even for livestock. In my own practice, contour trenches and bunds have been effective in slowing down runoff and allowing water to percolate into the soil.

Rooftop Rainwater Harvesting

Rooftop rainwater harvesting is a method where rainwater is collected from roof surfaces, typically via gutters and downspouts, and then stored in tanks or reservoirs. The quality of this water is usually higher, making it suitable for a variety of uses, including domestic purposes. It's particularly useful in urban areas, where ground space for water harvesting is limited.

Disadvantages and Limitations

Storage and Purification Challenges

One of the key challenges with rainwater harvesting is the need for adequate storage capacity. Large volumes of water may need to be stored for use during dry periods, requiring significant space and investment in storage infrastructure. Additionally, harvested rainwater may contain contaminants, necessitating purification or filtration systems before it can be used for certain purposes.

Legal and Regulatory Issues

In some regions, there are legal and regulatory hurdles associated with rainwater harvesting. Rights to rainwater and the impact of harvesting on groundwater recharge and downstream water availability can lead to restrictions or the need for permits. Navigating these legalities is an important aspect of setting up a rainwater harvesting system.

Global Examples of Rainwater Harvesting

Case Studies from Various Countries

In Australia, where water scarcity is a common issue, rainwater harvesting is widely practiced in both rural and urban areas. Households and farms use rainwater tanks to store water for domestic and agricultural use. In Rajasthan, India, traditional rainwater harvesting structures have revived water availability in this arid region, transforming the socio-economic landscape.

Success Stories and Challenges

In Thailand, the government's promotion of rainwater tanks in rural areas has significantly improved water security for farmers. However, challenges such as maintenance of storage tanks and changing rainfall patterns due to climate change continue to be areas of concern.

Sustainability Assessment

Environmental Impact

Rainwater harvesting has a positive environmental impact. It reduces dependency on groundwater and surface water, decreases soil erosion and runoff, and can enhance biodiversity in dry areas. Moreover, it reduces the energy consumption associated with pumping and distributing water from centralized systems.

Long-term Viability

The long-term viability of rainwater harvesting depends on factors like rainfall patterns, system maintenance, and community engagement. In regions with decreasing rainfall due to climate change, rainwater harvesting may become less feasible. However, with proper design, maintenance, and adaptive management, rainwater harvesting can be a sustainable solution for water scarcity for many years.

Soil Moisture Monitoring

Understanding and managing soil moisture is crucial in agriculture. This section will explore the various methods and tools used for soil moisture monitoring, its importance, and the latest innovations in the field.

Techniques for Measuring Soil Moisture

Gravimetric Method

The gravimetric method is one of the most basic yet accurate techniques for measuring soil moisture. It involves taking a soil sample, weighing it, drying it in an oven to remove all moisture, and then weighing it again. The difference in weight gives the moisture content. This method, while precise, is labor-intensive and not feasible for real-time monitoring over large areas.

Tensiometers

Tensiometers measure the tension or suction force with which water is held in the soil, providing an indication of the soil's moisture content. They consist of a water-filled tube with a porous ceramic tip that is placed in the soil. As the soil dries, water is pulled out of the tensiometer, creating a vacuum that is measured on a gauge. Tensiometers are particularly useful in sandy soils and for surface-level measurements.

Neutron Moisture Meters

Neutron moisture meters use the principle of neutron scattering to measure soil moisture. A source emits fast neutrons, which are slowed down when they collide with hydrogen atoms, primarily from water molecules in the soil. The slowed-down (thermal) neutrons are then detected and counted. The count is directly related to the amount of water in the soil. This method allows for deep soil moisture measurements and is highly accurate, but it requires specialized equipment and training.

Capacitance Probes

Capacitance probes measure the dielectric constant of the soil, which changes with moisture content. These probes are inserted into the soil and can provide continuous, real-time data on soil moisture at various depths. They are less disruptive than other methods and can be connected to data loggers for remote monitoring, making them highly suitable for precision agriculture.

Importance of Soil Moisture Monitoring

Optimizing Water Use

Accurate soil moisture monitoring helps in optimizing irrigation schedules, ensuring that crops receive the right amount of water at the right time. This can significantly reduce water wastage and lower irrigation costs.

Enhancing Crop Growth

Proper soil moisture is critical for healthy plant growth. By monitoring soil moisture levels, farmers can prevent stress conditions caused by both under and over-watering, leading to better crop yields and quality.

Preventing Over-Irrigation and Water Waste

Over-irrigation not only wastes water but also leaches essential nutrients from the soil, increases the risk of disease, and can lead to poor root development. Soil moisture monitoring allows for more precise water application, preventing these negative impacts.

Innovations in Soil Moisture Detection

Advanced Sensors and Technology

Recent advancements have led to the development of more sophisticated soil moisture sensors that are more accurate, durable, and easier to integrate with other technologies. Some sensors now come with wireless connectivity, enabling easy data collection and analysis.

Remote Sensing Techniques

Remote sensing, using satellites or drones, can provide soil moisture data over large areas. These techniques are particularly useful for large-scale agricultural operations and in assessing regional water balances.

Integration with Irrigation Systems

The integration of soil moisture sensors with automated irrigation systems represents a significant advancement. This allows for dynamic adjustment of irrigation based on real-time soil moisture data, enhancing water use efficiency and crop health.

Devices and Tools for Soil Moisture Monitoring

Description and Functions

Modern soil moisture devices range from simple tensiometers to advanced multisensor systems. For instance, smart soil moisture sensors can now measure temperature, electrical conductivity, and even nutrient levels in addition to moisture.

Accessibility and Cost Considerations

While advanced sensors offer more features, they also come with higher costs. However, with the growing emphasis on precision agriculture, these tools are becoming more accessible. Cost-effective options, like basic tensiometers or capacitance probes, are still available and provide significant benefits.

Conclusion

As we conclude our exploration of water management in agriculture, it becomes evident that this is a dynamic and critical field, one that intertwines the threads of sustainability, technology, and traditional knowledge.

The future of water management in agriculture looks promising yet challenging. With the increasing demands of a growing global population and the uncertainties posed by climate change, efficient water management is more crucial than ever. We are stepping into an era where the integration of technology and sustainable practices will define the success of agricultural endeavors.

Advancements in technology, such as AI, IoT (Internet of Things), and remote sensing, are set to revolutionize water management. These technologies can provide real-time data, predictive analytics, and more precise control over irrigation practices, making water use more efficient and sustainable. Furthermore, the growing awareness of climate change impacts is leading to a greater emphasis on conservation practices, such as rainwater harvesting and the use of drought-resistant crop varieties.

Yet, embracing these changes requires a collective effort. Farmers, scientists, policymakers, and communities must work together to implement and support sustainable water management practices. Continued research and investment in water-efficient technologies, along with education and training for farmers, are imperative for this transition.

The journey toward sustainable water management in agriculture is a shared responsibility. We must all contribute to conserving this vital resource while ensuring food security and environmental health.

1. **For Farmers and Gardeners:** Embrace efficient irrigation systems, practice soil moisture monitoring, and adopt rainwater harvesting where feasible. Stay informed about the latest technologies and techniques, and don't hesitate to seek support or training.
2. **For Consumers:** Support sustainable agriculture by choosing products from farms that practice efficient water management. Your purchasing decisions can drive change in the agricultural sector.

3. **For Policymakers and Industry Leaders:** Invest in research and development of sustainable agricultural technologies. Create policies and incentives that encourage water conservation and support farmers in transitioning to more sustainable practices.
4. **For the Community and Educators:** Raise awareness about the importance of water conservation in agriculture. Educate the younger generations and involve them in sustainable practices, creating a ripple effect for future change.

In summary, the future of agriculture depends on how effectively we manage our water resources today. It's a balance of harnessing technological advancements while honoring and learning from traditional practices. Through collective effort and commitment, we can ensure a sustainable, water-efficient future for agriculture, securing food supplies for generations to come and preserving the health of our planet.

Chapter Five — Implementing Regenerative Practices

As a farmer who has long embraced the soil under my feet and the crops that spring from it, I've come to understand the profound relationship between the land we cultivate and the methods we employ. Regenerative agriculture isn't just a set of techniques; it's a philosophy, a way of life that nurtures and replenishes the very ground that feeds us. In this chapter, we'll delve into the heart of regenerative practices, exploring their essence and how they can transform both small-scale farms and home gardens.

Regenerative agriculture goes beyond mere sustainability; it aims to actively rejuvenate the soil, enhancing its fertility and health and, by extension, the health of the plants and ecosystems it supports. It's about creating a closed-loop system where each element supports and enriches the others. For instance, by using no-till farming methods, we not only conserve soil structure but also build its organic matter, making it more fertile and resilient.

But what does this look like in practice? Imagine a farm where the fields aren't plowed year after year, where the soil isn't turned and disrupted but instead is covered with a rich blanket of organic matter. Here, the soil is alive with microorganisms, earthworms, and fungi, all working together to create a nutrient-rich environment for crops to flourish. In the sections that follow, we'll explore how practices like no-till farming, agroforestry, and natural pest management contribute to this vibrant agricultural tapestry.

One of the key aspects of regenerative practices is the diversity they introduce. By integrating different plant species, including trees and shrubs, into our farming systems, as seen in agroforestry, we not only improve the biodiversity of our farms but also enhance the resilience of our crops to pests and diseases. This approach can also provide additional income sources, from timber to fruit, nuts, and other non-timber forest products.

Pest management in regenerative agriculture isn't about waging war against insects and weeds with synthetic chemicals. Instead, it involves creating a balanced ecosystem where natural predators and beneficial insects keep harmful pest populations in check. It's about understanding the roles these creatures play and how we can support their existence to our advantage.

As we progress through this chapter, we'll uncover the hows and whys of these practices. We'll look at the practicalities of transitioning to no-till farming, the steps to integrate agroforestry into your farm or garden, and the ways to harness nature's own mechanisms for pest management. Each section is peppered with real-life examples, practical tips, and the wisdom gained from farmers who have walked this path.

Embarking on the journey of regenerative agriculture is not just about improving our individual plots of land; it's about contributing to a larger movement, one that seeks to heal and rejuvenate our planet's exhausted agricultural landscapes. As we explore these practices together, remember that each step taken is a seed sown for a more fertile, resilient, and sustainable future.

No-Till Farming

No-till farming is a revolutionary agricultural practice that contrasts sharply with traditional tillage methods. It involves planting crops directly into the residue of previous crops without plowing or disturbing the soil. This method has emerged as a sustainable alternative to conventional tillage, offering profound benefits to both the soil and the environment.

Comparison with Traditional Till Farming

Traditional till farming, a practice that dates back centuries, involves turning the soil to prepare seedbeds, control weeds, and incorporate fertilizers or organic matter. While effective in the short term, this method disrupts soil structure, accelerates erosion, and reduces soil fertility over time. No-till farming, in contrast, maintains the integrity of the soil by avoiding disruption. This approach helps in preserving the soil's organic matter and structure, making it a more sustainable option.

Benefits of No-Till for Soil Health

No-till farming significantly enhances soil health. It increases organic matter content and improves soil structure, leading to greater fertility and productivity. The undisturbed soil also supports a diverse and active ecosystem of microorganisms, beneficial insects, and fungi, crucial for nutrient cycling and soil health. Additionally, no-till farming aids in carbon sequestration, helping to mitigate climate change.

Transformative Effects on Farms

No-till farming has transformative effects on both the micro and macro levels of agricultural ecosystems.

Soil Structure and Fertility Improvements

The structure of soil under no-till practices undergoes substantial improvement. Soil under no-till retains a natural stratification and aeration that benefits root growth and nutrient uptake. The improved soil structure also enhances the soil's water-holding capacity, making crops more resilient to droughts and reducing the need for irrigation.

In terms of fertility, no-till farming helps in building up organic matter. This organic matter acts as a reservoir of nutrients that are slowly released to plants. Over time, no-till fields often show higher levels of key nutrients like nitrogen, phosphorus, and potassium compared to tilled fields.

Water Conservation and Erosion Control

No-till farming is exemplary in its ability to conserve water and control erosion. The crop residues left on the soil surface reduce water evaporation and improve soil moisture retention. This mulch-like layer also protects the soil from the impact of raindrops, which can dislodge soil particles and lead to erosion. Over time, no-till fields demonstrate significantly reduced rates of both water and wind erosion, contributing to better water quality in adjacent waterways and reduced sedimentation.

Practical Methods for Implementing No-Till

Implementing no-till farming requires careful planning and a shift in traditional farming practices.

Transition Strategies from Traditional Tillage

Transitioning to no-till can be challenging, particularly for farms long accustomed to conventional tillage. A gradual approach is often recommended. Begin by reducing the depth and frequency of tillage, allowing the soil and its ecosystem to adjust. It's also important to experiment with different crop residues and cover crops to find the best combination for soil cover and health.

During the transition, soil testing becomes crucial. Regularly monitor changes in soil composition, moisture levels, and crop health to fine-tune the approach. It's also vital to educate oneself about the nuances of no-till, from understanding the biology of the soil ecosystem to the specifics of no-till equipment.

Equipment and Technology Used in No-Till Farming

Specialized equipment is essential for successful no-till farming. Key among these is the no-till drill or planter, designed to plant seeds in undisturbed soil. These implements must efficiently cut through crop residue, place seeds at the correct depth, and ensure good seed-to-soil contact. Modern no-till drills are equipped with features like disc openers and seed firmers to facilitate this process.

Additionally, advancements in precision agriculture technologies, such as GPS-guided planting systems and soil moisture sensors, can significantly enhance the effectiveness of no-till farming.

Managing Crop Residues and Soil Cover

Effective residue management is central to no-till farming. Crop residues are left on the field post-harvest, which helps in protecting the soil surface. Deciding which crops to grow and how to manage their residues is a critical aspect of this system. For instance, residues from crops like corn and wheat provide excellent soil cover but might require specific strategies for decomposition.

The use of cover crops is another crucial aspect of no-till farming. Cover crops like clover, vetch, and rye can be grown between main crop cycles to protect and enrich the soil. These crops help suppress weeds, prevent soil erosion, and enhance soil fertility through nitrogen fixation and organic matter addition.

In conclusion, no-till farming is not just an agricultural practice but a sustainable approach to land stewardship. By understanding and implementing its principles, farmers and gardeners can contribute to healthier soils, increased biodiversity, and a more resilient agricultural system. The transition to no-till may require patience and adaptation, but the long-term benefits for the soil, the environment, and the farmer are immense.

Agroforestry Integration

Agroforestry, a practice blending agriculture and forestry, creates systems where trees or shrubs are grown around or among crops or pastureland. This integration forms a symbiotic relationship between different plant species, offering various ecological and economic benefits.

Agroforestry is founded on the principle of creating a more biodiverse, productive, and sustainable land-use system. It involves the intentional integration of trees and shrubs into crop and animal farming systems to create environmental, economic, and social benefits. The trees in these systems can provide shade, act as windbreaks, and contribute to the ecological health of the area by supporting diverse wildlife.

Historically, agroforestry has been practiced in various forms around the world, often as a traditional land-use system in many indigenous communities. Today, it is being adopted and adapted for modern applications, driven by the need for sustainable agricultural practices. Modern agroforestry includes alley cropping, silvopasture, forest farming, and riparian buffers, each tailored to specific environmental and economic goals.

Agroforestry's Impact on Ecosystems and Crops

Agroforestry has a profound positive impact on ecosystems and the crops grown within them.

Biodiversity Enhancement and Microclimate Regulation:

The integration of trees and crops leads to enhanced biodiversity. Trees provide habitat for a range of organisms, which contribute to a balanced ecosystem. They also help regulate the microclimate around crops, reducing temperature extremes, which can be particularly beneficial in regions facing climate variability.

Soil Health and Nutrient Cycling Benefits:

Trees in agroforestry systems play a vital role in improving soil health. Their roots help in preventing soil erosion and improve soil structure. They also contribute to nutrient cycling, with some tree species being capable of nitrogen fixation, which enriches the soil naturally.

Agroforestry for Sustainability:

Agroforestry is a key component in the movement toward more sustainable land use.

Contribution to Sustainable Land Use:

By integrating trees and crops, agroforestry creates a more sustainable use of land. It allows for the simultaneous production of crops and tree products, maximizing land use efficiency. This approach can be particularly beneficial in areas where land resources are limited.

Economic and Environmental Benefits:

Economically, agroforestry can diversify income sources for farmers, providing both agricultural and forest products. Environmentally, it contributes to carbon sequestration, biodiversity conservation, and the sustainable management of natural resources.

Benefits to Trees and Crop Fields:

The synergy between trees and crops in agroforestry systems leads to mutual benefits.

Synergistic Relationships in Agroforestry Systems:

Trees and crops in agroforestry systems interact beneficially. For example, deep-rooted trees can bring up nutrients from lower soil layers, making them available to crops. Additionally, the shade provided by trees can reduce water loss in crops and protect them from extreme weather.

Case Studies Demonstrating Agroforestry Success:

Numerous case studies worldwide illustrate the success of agroforestry. For example, in Kenya, farmers practicing agroforestry with nitrogen-fixing trees have seen significant increases in maize yields. In the United States, alley cropping systems, where crops are grown between rows of trees, have proven successful in diversifying farm income and improving wildlife habitat.

In summary, agroforestry represents a promising intersection of agriculture and forestry, offering a sustainable approach to land management. By understanding and adopting agroforestry practices, farmers can improve the health of their land, increase biodiversity, and enjoy a more diverse income stream, all while contributing to the overall health of the environment.

Pest Management through Natural Means

Natural pest management, often termed Integrated Pest Management (IPM), is a holistic approach focusing on the long-term prevention of pests or their damage through a combination of techniques such as biological control, habitat manipulation, and the use of resistant varieties. The primary principle is to create a balanced ecosystem where pests are managed through natural processes rather than relying solely on chemical interventions.

Contrast with Synthetic Pest Management Methods:

Unlike synthetic methods that often involve the use of chemical pesticides to eliminate pests, natural pest management prioritizes ecological balance and sustainability. Chemical pesticides can be effective in the short term but often have detrimental effects such as resistance to pests, harm to non-target organisms (like pollinators), and environmental pollution. Natural pest control, on the other hand, emphasizes maintaining the health of the soil, plants, and beneficial organisms, reducing the reliance on harmful chemicals.

Natural Biological Methods for Pest Control:

Use of Predators, Parasites, and Beneficial Insects:

A cornerstone of natural pest management is the use of biological control agents. This includes encouraging or introducing predators (like ladybugs and lacewings), parasites (such as certain wasp species), and beneficial insects (like ground beetles) that naturally keep pest populations in check. For instance, ladybugs are voracious consumers of aphids, a common pest in many gardens and farms. Implementing practices like planting flowering shrubs or hedgerows can attract and sustain these beneficial organisms.

Plant-based Pest Repellents and Biological Insecticides:

Natural pest management also involves using plant-based repellents and biological insecticides. Certain plants, like marigolds or garlic, naturally repel specific pests and can be intercropped with other crops. Biological insecticides, such as Bacillus thuringiensis (Bt), a naturally occurring bacteria, can target specific pests without harming beneficial insects, a significant advantage over broad-spectrum synthetic pesticides.

The Role of Natural Insecticides:

Definition and Types of Natural Insecticides:

Natural insecticides are substances derived from natural sources (like plants, bacteria, and minerals) used to control pests. They include botanical insecticides like neem oil, which disrupts the life cycle of pests, and mineral-based products like diatomaceous earth, which physically damages pest exoskeletons.

Advantages and Limitations of Natural Insecticides:

The primary advantage of natural insecticides is their reduced environmental impact and safety for non-target organisms, including humans. They often break down faster in the environment, reducing residual effects. However, they may have limitations in terms of shelf life and variable effectiveness depending on environmental conditions and sometimes require more frequent application than synthetic alternatives.

Addressing Severe Pest Infestations Naturally:

Strategies for Managing Significant Pest Outbreaks:

Dealing with severe pest infestations naturally requires a multi-pronged approach. One strategy is crop rotation, which disrupts pest life cycles. Another effective method is the use of trap crops planted to attract pests away from the main crop. Physical barriers, such as row covers, can also protect crops during critical growth periods. In some cases, introducing or encouraging natural predators and parasites in greater numbers can help bring a pest outbreak under control.

Integration of Natural Pest Management with Other Farming Practices:

Natural pest management works best when integrated with other sustainable farming practices. This includes maintaining healthy soil (as healthy plants are more resistant to pests), practicing diversity through polyculture or companion planting (which can confuse or repel pests), and monitoring pest populations regularly to make informed management decisions.

Conclusion

As we draw this chapter to a close, it's clear that the path to sustainable and regenerative agriculture is both challenging and rewarding. The practices we've discussed are not mere techniques; they are a testament to a growing consciousness about the delicate balance between human activity and the natural world.

Natural pest management is a critical component of sustainable agriculture, focusing on long-term pest prevention and ecological balance. By understanding and implementing these methods, farmers and gardeners can effectively manage pests in an environmentally friendly manner, contributing to the health of the ecosystem and the safety of food production. This approach requires patience, observation, and a willingness to work with nature's rhythms and cycles, but the rewards are a more resilient and vibrant farming system.

Farmers and agriculturists stand at the forefront of this transformation. They are the stewards of the land, tasked with the critical responsibility of reshaping agriculture into a sustainable practice. Their role extends beyond food production; they are guardians of soil health, biodiversity, and ecological balance.

By embracing sustainable practices, as detailed in this guide, farmers can revitalize the land, conserve resources, and contribute to a healthier environment. The adoption of no-till farming, for instance, requires a paradigm shift in understanding soil as a living ecosystem. Similarly, integrating agroforestry and implementing natural pest management are reflections of a deepened respect for nature's processes and cycles.

Moreover, farmers play a crucial role in preserving traditional knowledge and blending it with modern innovations. Their insights and experiences are invaluable in evolving and adapting regenerative practices that are context-specific, acknowledging the unique challenges and opportunities of different agricultural landscapes.

Future Directions and Emerging Trends in Regenerative Practices

Looking ahead, the future of regenerative agriculture is poised at the intersection of tradition and innovation. We are witnessing a growing trend toward technology-driven practices, such as precision agriculture, which harnesses data and technology to make farming more efficient and less resource-intensive. However, the heart of sustainability lies in recognizing and valuing the intrinsic connection between human well-being and ecological health.

Emerging trends include the integration of more sophisticated, ecologically based pest management strategies, the development of crops better suited to local ecosystems, and a greater emphasis on permaculture principles. Additionally, there's a rising movement toward community-supported agriculture (CSA) and urban farming initiatives, which not only bring fresh, locally grown food to urban areas but also foster a deeper connection between consumers and the sources of their food.

Climate change and environmental degradation will continue to challenge farmers, requiring adaptive and resilient farming practices. The use of agroforestry and diversified farming systems is likely to gain more traction as effective strategies to combat these challenges.

In essence, the future of agriculture is not just about producing food; it's about nurturing the earth that sustains us. It's a journey of learning, adapting, and evolving with a focus on long-term ecological balance. As farmers, gardeners, and consumers, our collective efforts in embracing regenerative practices will shape the legacy we leave for future generations – a legacy of fertile soils, diverse ecosystems, and a harmonious relationship with our planet.

Chapter Six — Profit Optimization Techniques

In the world of small-scale farming and home gardening, efficiency is more than a buzzword — it's the cornerstone of our livelihood. I've walked this path long enough to understand that the difference between a bountiful year and a struggling one often lies in how effectively we manage our resources. Reducing costs is not merely a matter of financial savings; it's about creating a sustainable practice that can withstand the ups and downs of agricultural life.

Every decision, from the type of seed you plant to the method of pest control you choose, impacts your bottom line. In this journey, we're aiming to unearth ways to maximize outputs while minimizing inputs, ensuring that each drop of water, each grain of soil, and each hour of labor contributes positively to our end goal: a profitable and sustainable farming practice.

Profitable Farming Practices: Evaluating the Profit Margins of Different Farming Methods

The core of profitable farming lies in understanding and optimizing profit margins. Consider two fundamental elements: revenue and costs. Revenue comes from the sale of your crops or produce, while costs are what you spend to grow them. To maximize profits, we need to increase revenue while minimizing costs.

For instance, let's examine intercropping and monoculture. Intercropping, where we grow two or more crops in proximity, can lead to a higher yield per unit area, increasing revenue. It also diversifies risk; if one crop fails, you still have others to fall back on. Monoculture, or growing a single crop, might seem simpler but can be riskier and often more resource-intensive.

Case Studies: Examples of Successful Profitable Farming

Let's take real-life examples. John, a farmer in Nebraska, adopted no-till farming. By not disturbing the soil, he was able to significantly reduce fuel and equipment costs. His soil's health improved over time, leading to higher and more sustainable yields.

Then there's Maria from California. She embraced integrated pest management (IPM), using beneficial insects and biocontrols. This natural method reduced her reliance on chemical pesticides, cutting costs and appealing to the growing market for eco-friendly produce.

Maximizing Efficiency in Agriculture

Techniques for Increasing Crop Yield

Yield is the golden word in our farming lexicon. But how do we increase it sustainably? First, understand the needs of your crops. Select varieties that are suited to your climate and soil type. Employ crop rotation, which not only prevents nutrient depletion in the soil but also disrupts pest and disease cycles.

Secondly, consider soil health. Regular soil testing can guide your fertilization strategy, ensuring that you're not over or under-applying nutrients. Compost and green manure can improve soil fertility and structure, leading to better water retention and healthier plants.

Reducing Wastage and Resource Management

Waste reduction and resource management are pivotal. Implementing a robust composting system turns waste into a resource. Additionally, water management is crucial. Methods like drip irrigation and mulching reduce water usage and costs. Collecting and storing rainwater can also provide a cost-effective irrigation source.

Cost vs. Benefit Analysis

Transitioning to organic farming involves higher initial costs but can be more profitable in the long run. Organic methods reduce reliance on chemical inputs, which can be expensive. Organic produce generally sells at a premium price, increasing potential revenue.

Start small when transitioning to organic. Test it on a part of your farm and compare the results. Monitor everything from pest occurrences to yield sizes. This measured approach helps in understanding the practical and financial implications before fully committing.

Consumer Demand for Organic Produce

The demand for organic produce is rising steadily, driven by health and environmental concerns. This trend presents an opportunity for higher profit margins. Organic markets, CSA

(Community Supported Agriculture) programs, and farm-to-table restaurants are excellent outlets for organic produce.

Comparative Analysis of Farming Methods

Traditional vs. Modern Techniques

Balancing traditional wisdom with modern innovation is key. Traditional methods, such as crop rotation and biological pest control, are time-tested and sustainable. Modern techniques like precision farming use technology to optimize resource use, which can lead to significant cost savings. The best approach often lies in a combination of both, tailored to your specific circumstances.

Impact on Long-Term Profitability

The sustainability of any farming method is crucial to its long-term profitability. Practices that preserve soil health, conserve resources and maintain ecological balance not only reduce costs but also ensure that the farm remains productive for years to come.

Through these expanded insights into cost-effective farming methods, we delve into the nuances of what makes a farm both profitable and sustainable. Each decision we make as farmers and gardeners should be guided by these principles, ensuring that we're not only reaping the benefits today but also paving the way for a fruitful future.

Marketing and Sales Tactics for Agricultural Products

Marketing and sales tactics for agricultural products are crucial for bridging the gap between farmers and consumers. These strategies involve understanding market trends, consumer preferences, and effective communication channels to promote farm products effectively. In the agriculture sector, where products are often perishable, and the market can be volatile, skilled marketing ensures that farmers can secure better prices and reduce waste by aligning production with market demand. Effective sales tactics help in expanding market reach, building customer relationships, and ensuring long-term sustainability for farmers. In essence, adept marketing and sales are vital for the economic viability of agricultural endeavors and for meeting global food demands.

Identifying Your Market

Farming isn't just about planting seeds and harvesting crops. It's also about knowing who's going to buy your produce. This is where market research comes in. Take time to understand different types of customers and their preferences — are they looking for organic vegetables, heirloom fruits, or perhaps exotic herbs? Local markets might favor fresh, farm-to-table produce, whereas others might be more interested in processed goods like jams or pickles.

One method is to visit local markets and grocery stores, talk to customers, and see what's selling. Are there trends in what people are buying? What are they looking for that they can't find? This information is golden. You can also use online tools, surveys, and even social media to get insights into customer preferences.

Branding and Positioning in Agriculture

Your farm is more than just a place where crops grow; it's a brand. Developing a strong brand can set you apart in the crowded market. Start by defining what makes your farm unique. Is it your commitment to organic practices, a family heritage in farming, or perhaps a specific type of crop you're known for?

Create a logo and a slogan that reflects your farm's identity. Use these on your packaging, website, business cards, and any marketing materials. This consistent branding helps build recognition and customer trust. Remember, your farm's brand isn't just what you sell; it's the story you tell.

Eight Key Marketing Strategies for Farmers

Digital Marketing Techniques

In today's digital age, having an online presence is crucial. A simple, user-friendly website showcasing your farm and produce can attract customers far and wide. Social media platforms like Instagram, Facebook, and Twitter are powerful tools to engage with your audience. Share stories from your farm, updates about your produce, and even behind-the-scenes glimpses into the farming life.

Consider email marketing. Regular newsletters with updates about your farm, upcoming harvests, and special offers can keep your customers engaged and informed. Also, learn the basics of Search Engine Optimization (SEO) to ensure your website shows up in relevant searches.

Direct-to-Consumer Sales Approaches

Direct-to-consumer sales remove the middleman, allowing you to build a direct relationship with your customers. This can be achieved through various channels like farmers' markets, CSA (Community Supported Agriculture) programs or farm stands.

CSA programs, where customers pay upfront for a share of your harvest, provide upfront capital and guarantee a market for your produce. Hosting farm tours and pick-your-own events can also draw people to your farm, creating a unique experience that can foster loyalty and word-of-mouth marketing.

Leveraging Technology for Sales

Technology has revolutionized how we sell products. Online sales platforms, mobile payment options, and even simple technologies like QR codes can make buying from your farm easy and accessible.

Online marketplaces specifically for local produce can broaden your customer base. Additionally, implementing farm management software can streamline your sales process, track inventory, and manage customer orders more efficiently.

Building Customer Loyalty

Loyal customers are the backbone of any business. Create loyalty programs like discounts for returning customers or referral bonuses. Personal touches like handwritten thank-you notes, small gifts with large purchases, or even a loyalty card can go a long way in building a strong customer relationship.

Organizing community events or workshops on your farm can also strengthen this bond. Sharing knowledge about farming practices or cooking demonstrations using your produce can enhance customer engagement.

Creative Advertising Methods

In the world of advertising, creativity is king. Traditional methods like flyers and local newspaper ads have their place, but don't be afraid to think outside the box. Partner with local businesses to promote each other's products or sponsor community events to increase visibility.

Social media contests or giveaways can create buzz around your farm. Collaborating with influencers or bloggers who align with your brand values can also introduce your farm to a broader audience.

Engagement with Local Communities

Engaging with your local community establishes your farm as a trusted local business. Participate in local fairs, school programs, or community gardens. Offer to speak at local events about sustainable farming or healthy eating.

Establishing strong ties with your community not only builds a loyal customer base but also creates a network of support and collaboration, vital for small-scale farmers and home gardeners.

Identifying Lucrative Marketplaces

Today's market is a blend of physical and digital. While traditional marketplaces like farmers' markets and grocery stores are important, online marketplaces are increasingly becoming popular. Many customers enjoy the convenience of online shopping.

Evaluate the pros and cons of each. Online marketplaces might require a digital marketing strategy and logistics for shipping, but they can reach a wider audience. Physical marketplaces, on the other hand, offer the advantage of personal interaction and immediate sales.

Collaborating with Retailers and Wholesalers

Building relationships with local retailers and wholesalers can open doors to new markets. They can provide a consistent demand and larger orders. However, it's important to maintain a balance. Direct-to-consumer sales often yield higher profit margins, but wholesalers can take a significant amount of produce off your hands with minimal hassle.

When negotiating with retailers or wholesalers, ensure that you're getting a fair price for your produce. Understand the terms of the agreement and ensure it's beneficial for both parties.

Implementing effective marketing and sales strategies is as vital as growing the crop itself. As farmers, embracing these practices not only helps us thrive in a competitive market but also connects us more closely with our consumers, creating a symbiotic relationship where everyone benefits. Remember, the goal is not just to sell but to build a community around our produce, where each fruit and vegetable tells the story of our dedication and hard work.

Planting the Most Profitable Produce

Planting the most profitable produce involves strategic selection of crops based on factors like market demand, climate suitability, and yield potential. This approach is critical for maximizing returns from agricultural investments. Profitable farming demands understanding consumer trends and preferences, especially for high-value or niche market products. Additionally, considering the cost of inputs versus potential market price is essential in decision-making. High-value crops often require more intensive management but can offer significantly higher returns. Moreover, adapting to local environmental conditions and sustainable farming practices can enhance yield and quality, further driving profitability. In essence, choosing the right produce to plant is a blend of market savvy, agronomic knowledge, and environmental stewardship, pivotal for successful and sustainable agriculture.

Trends in High-Profit Crops

In farming, like any other business, understanding market trends and consumer preferences is critical. It's not just about growing what we like; it's about growing what sells. For instance, organic produce has seen a surge in demand over recent years. Consumers are increasingly health-conscious and environmentally aware, seeking out organic fruits, vegetables, and even grains.

To tap into these trends, conduct market research. This could involve visiting local markets, surveying customers, or analyzing data from agricultural reports. Look for patterns in what people buy. Are leafy greens more popular? Is there a demand for exotic fruits? This information can guide you in deciding what crops to plant.

Adapting to Climate and Regional Conditions

Choosing crops that suit your local climate and soil conditions is just as important as following market trends. Certain crops thrive in specific conditions. For example, if you're in a region with a dry climate, consider drought-resistant crops like sorghum or millet. These crops not only have a better chance of thriving but also might have less competition in the market, fetching a higher price.

Additionally, consider the length of your growing season. If you have a short season, focus on crops that mature quickly. Conversely, if your growing season is longer, you might have the opportunity to grow crops that require a longer time to mature, potentially leading to higher yields and profits.

Price Elasticity and Crop Selection

Price elasticity refers to how the demand for a product changes with its price. Some crops are inelastic, meaning that demand doesn't change much regardless of price fluctuations – staples like potatoes and rice are good examples. Others, like specialty herbs or exotic fruits, are more elastic; demand can decrease significantly if prices rise.

Understanding this concept can help you choose which crops to grow. Inelastic crops offer more stable demand, while elastic crops can yield higher profits but come with greater risk. Balance is key. It might be wise to grow a mix of both types, ensuring a steady income while also taking advantage of potentially higher profits from more elastic crops.

Responding to Market Fluctuations

Market prices for crops can fluctuate due to various factors — changes in consumer trends, weather conditions affecting harvests, or even global events impacting supply chains. As a farmer, staying informed and being able to pivot quickly is crucial.

One strategy is to diversify your crops. Don't put all your eggs in one basket. If you're growing a high-value but volatile crop, also grow something more stable. This way, if the market for one crop crashes, you have a backup. Another approach is to have a contingency plan — for instance, if a particular crop's price drops, can it be processed or stored for selling later?

Strategies for Competitive Pricing

Setting the right price for your produce can be the difference between profit and loss. Understand your costs first — this includes the cost of seeds, fertilizers, water, labor, and any other inputs. Then, add a margin for profit. However, be aware of the market rate. If your prices are too high, your produce might not sell. If they're too low, you might not cover your costs.

Competitive pricing also involves knowing when to sell. Sometimes, holding off for a few weeks can lead to better prices, especially if there's a seasonal surge in demand or a drop in supply.

Understanding the Psychology of Buyers

Buying decisions are not always rational. Factors like freshness, appearance, and even packaging can influence buyers. Many consumers are willing to pay more for produce that looks better or comes in eco-friendly packaging. Additionally, storytelling can be a powerful tool. Share the story of your farm, your practices, and the quality of your produce. This emotional connection can make consumers more willing to pay a premium.

Selecting Crops for Maximum Profit

High-Demand Crops Analysis

Research and identify crops that are currently in high demand and offer good profit margins. These might include specialty vegetables for local gourmet restaurants, organic fruits for health-conscious consumers, or even medicinal herbs.

Stay updated with agricultural extensions, market bulletins, and trade publications. These sources often provide valuable information about which crops are in demand and emerging market trends.

Rotation and Diversification for Sustainability

Crop rotation and diversification are not just good agricultural practices; they are also smart business strategies. Rotating crops can improve soil health and reduce pest problems, leading to higher yields and, subsequently, higher profits.

Diversification, on the other hand, spreads risk. If one crop doesn't perform well, you're not entirely at a loss. It also allows you to take advantage of different market trends and seasonal demands. Plus, a diverse farm can attract a wider range of customers, from those looking for common produce to those seeking something unique.

Selecting the right crops to plant is a delicate balance of understanding market demands, adapting to environmental conditions, and managing economic risks. It's about being agile and responsive to the market while staying true to the realities of your land and its capabilities. In the end, the goal is to cultivate a farm that is not only profitable but also sustainable and resilient in the face of an ever-changing agricultural landscape.

Diversifying Income Streams in Agriculture

In today's farming, relying solely on income from selling crops or livestock may not be sufficient for long-term financial stability. Diversification is key. Beyond the traditional sale of produce, there are various ways to generate revenue. These include agritourism, selling value-added products like jams or cheeses, offering educational workshops, and even renting out land.

Each of these streams has its own set of advantages and challenges. For instance, value-added products can significantly increase profit margins but require additional skills, resources, and possibly certifications. Agritourism can be lucrative, especially in areas close to urban centers, but it involves additional overheads and management skills.

Balancing Investment and Returns

When considering diversification, it's crucial to balance the initial investment against the potential returns. For example, starting a pick-your-own operation might require investing in visitor facilities and marketing. However, it can attract a steady stream of customers willing to pay a premium for the experience of harvesting their own food.

Similarly, venturing into processing agricultural produce into value-added products may require equipment and additional labor. Analyze the market demand, costs, potential pricing, and the time it will take to break even. A well-thought-out plan, considering both short-term and long-term returns, is essential.

Value-Added Products and Services

Turning raw produce into value-added products is a fantastic way to increase revenue. For instance, if you're growing tomatoes, consider making and selling tomato sauce, salsa, or sun-dried tomatoes. The key here is to identify products that align with your crop production and have a market demand.

Apart from food products, consider offering services like farm consulting or agritourism. If you have expertise in organic farming, soil health, or sustainable practices, you could offer consulting services to other farmers or individuals looking to start a garden.

Agricultural Tourism and Educational Programs

Agriculture tourism and educational programs are unique ways to diversify income. This could include farm stays, guided tours, or workshops on topics like beekeeping, canning, or organic gardening. These activities not only generate additional revenue but also help in building a community around your farm and promoting agricultural education.

Developing educational programs requires a deep understanding of your audience's interests. Tailor your programs to different groups — families might enjoy farm animal interactions, while adults may be interested in a farm-to-table cooking class.

Exploring Land Rental and Other Ventures

Land leasing can be a profitable venture, especially if you have more land than you can cultivate or if you are looking for a passive income stream. Leasing out land for farming, grazing, or even solar farms can provide a steady income.

However, it's important to understand the risks. The quality of your land could be impacted depending on how the lessee uses it. Drafting a detailed lease agreement that specifies the land use and maintenance expectations is crucial. Consider the long-term impact of the lease on your land's health and productivity.

Alternative Agricultural Business Models

Exploring alternative business models can also provide diverse income streams. For example, community-supported agriculture (CSA) models where consumers pay a subscription for a weekly or monthly supply of produce create a steady income stream and reduce marketing costs.

Another model is cooperative farming, where multiple farmers pool their resources (land, machinery, capital) to reduce costs and increase market presence. This can also open up opportunities for larger contracts, such as supplying to schools or hospitals, that might be unattainable for an individual small-scale farmer.

Diversifying income streams in agriculture is about finding creative and sustainable ways to utilize your farm's resources. Whether it's through value-added products, agritourism, land leasing, or exploring alternative business models, each option has the potential to enhance financial stability and resilience. Remember, the key to successful diversification is aligning these ventures with your core farming operations, market demands, and personal strengths. By doing so, not only do you safeguard your farm's financial health, but you also enrich the agricultural tapestry of your community.

Exploring Sustainable Agricultural Models

Sustainable agricultural models are innovative approaches aimed at achieving high productivity while ensuring environmental health and social equity. These models focus on efficient resource use, soil conservation, minimizing chemical inputs, and promoting biodiversity. They are vital in addressing the challenges of food security, climate change, and ecological sustainability. By integrating practices like organic farming, agroecology, and precision agriculture, sustainable models work toward a balanced, responsible, and long-term approach to farming that benefits both the planet and its inhabitants.

Integrated Farming Systems

An Integrated Farming System (IFS) represents a holistic approach to farming, where multiple agricultural activities are synergistically combined to enhance overall efficiency and sustainability. The core principle of IFS is that the waste of one component can be a resource for another. For example, in a well-designed IFS, livestock manure is used to fertilize crops, crop residues are utilized as fodder, and a pond for fish farming might be integrated into the system to help with irrigation and nutrient recycling.

This approach demands careful planning and a deep understanding of the ecological interactions within your farm. For instance, integrating livestock into crop farming requires knowledge about which animals are beneficial for your specific crops, understanding their feeding and grazing patterns, and managing their health in a way that doesn't harm your crops.

The benefits of IFS extend beyond just increased production efficiency. This approach can greatly enhance biodiversity on the farm, improve soil health, reduce dependency on chemical inputs, and offer multiple streams of income, which is crucial for financial resilience. However, transitioning to an IFS model requires time, effort, and often a shift in traditional farming practices. It may involve trial and error to find the right balance and combination of activities that work for your specific context.

Regenerative Agriculture Practices

Regenerative Agriculture is an approach focused on rehabilitating and enhancing the entire ecosystem of the farm. It's not just about sustaining; it's about actively improving soil health, water management, and biodiversity. Key practices in regenerative agriculture include:

1. **No-till farming:** This method avoids the turning of soil which disrupts soil structure and microbial life. Keeping the soil intact helps in carbon sequestration and improves soil health.
2. **Cover cropping:** Planting cover crops like clover or ryegrass in between harvests can prevent soil

erosion, enhance soil fertility, and manage weeds naturally.
3. **Rotational Grazing:** Rotating livestock across pastures not only prevents overgrazing but also aids in evenly distributing manure, a natural fertilizer.
4. **Permaculture:** This is a design system for creating sustainable human environments. In farming, it translates to creating diversified, self-sufficient agricultural systems that mimic natural ecosystems.

Implementing regenerative practices can initially be challenging, especially if your farm has been reliant on conventional methods. However, the long-term benefits, such as improved soil fertility, reduced input costs, and increased resilience to climate change, make it a worthwhile investment.

The Pillars of Sustainability in Agriculture

The Four Cs: Conservation, Community, Culture and Commerce

These four Cs form the foundational pillars of a sustainable agricultural system.

1. **Conservation:** This involves the careful management of natural resources such as soil, water, and biodiversity. Practices include reducing soil erosion, conserving water through efficient irrigation systems, and fostering biodiversity by maintaining natural habitats and planting a variety

of crops. It's not just about using resources wisely but also about actively improving them.
2. **Community:** Agriculture is deeply rooted in the community. This pillar emphasizes building strong, mutually beneficial relationships with local communities, fellow farmers, consumers, and local businesses. This can be achieved through community-supported agriculture (CSA) programs, farmer cooperatives, and local farmers' markets. A strong community connection ensures a robust support network, which is vital for the long-term sustainability of your farming enterprise.
3. **Culture:** This involves preserving traditional farming methods that are inherently sustainable while integrating them with innovative practices. It's about respecting the legacy and wisdom of traditional agricultural practices and learning from them. Culture in sustainable agriculture also means educating the next generation about the importance of sustainable farming and encouraging their participation.
4. **Commerce:** Sustainable agriculture must also be economically viable. This involves developing business models that are profitable while being ecologically and socially responsible. It means fair pricing, ethical labor practices, and considering the long-term economic viability of farming practices rather than just short-term gains.

The Five Cs: Climate, Customers, Crops, Conservation and Community

Adding to the previous four, the 5th C — Climate — is becoming increasingly critical.

1. **Climate:** This involves understanding the impacts of climate change on agriculture and implementing practices that not only reduce these impacts but also improve the farm's resilience. This could include selecting climate-resilient crop varieties, employing water conservation methods, and reducing the farm's carbon footprint.
2. **Customers:** Sustainable agriculture also pays close attention to customer needs and preferences, especially the growing demand for sustainable and ethically produced food. This involves direct communication with customers, understanding their preferences, and educating them about the benefits of sustainable agriculture.
3. **Crops:** The choice of crops plays a significant role in sustainability. This involves selecting crops suited to the local climate and soil, using seeds that require less water or are pest-resistant, and diversifying crops to ensure ecological balance and reduce risk.

Combining these pillars creates a robust framework for sustainable agriculture. But how do we put these principles into practice? In the next part, we will delve into the practical steps for transitioning to sustainable practices and explore some successful case studies. Let's continue with Part 3.

Implementing Sustainable Practices

The journey toward sustainable agriculture is a step-by-step process requiring commitment and gradual changes. Here's how you can start:

1. **Conduct a Farm Audit:** Begin with an evaluation of your current practices. Identify areas where improvements can be made, whether it's water usage, soil health, pest management, or energy efficiency.
2. **Set Achievable Goals:** Start with small, achievable goals. This could be something as simple as reducing water usage by a certain percentage or implementing a no-till practice in a portion of your land.
3. **Education and Training:** Educate yourself about sustainable practices. Attend workshops, webinars, or courses focused on sustainable agriculture. Training for you and your staff ensures everyone is on the same page and understands the importance of these changes.
4. **Implement Changes Gradually:** Implement new practices gradually. For example, if you're transitioning to organic farming, start with a small plot before converting your entire farm. This allows you to learn and adjust as you go.
5. **Monitor and Adjust:** Regularly monitor the outcomes of the changes you implement. Keep records of soil health, crop yields, water usage, and

any other relevant metrics. Use this data to adjust your practices and improve.
6. **Seek Support and Collaboration:** Don't hesitate to seek support from the agricultural community. This could include advice from other sustainable farmers, assistance from agricultural extension services, or collaboration with local research institutions.
7. **Engage with the Community:** Involve the local community in your journey. Host open days, workshops, or farm tours to educate the public about sustainable farming practices and the importance of supporting local agriculture.

Case Studies of Successful Sustainable Farms

1. Polyface Farm, Virginia, USA

Background: Polyface Farm, located in Virginia's Shenandoah Valley, is a family-owned, multi-generational farm known for its pioneering work in regenerative agriculture.

Practices Implemented:

Rotational Grazing: They use a system called "mob stocking," where cattle are moved frequently to fresh pasture, mimicking natural grazing patterns. This practice revitalizes the grass and soil, sequestering carbon and improving biodiversity.

Multi-species Integration: Chickens, pigs, and cattle are integrated into a symbiotic relationship. For example, chickens follow cattle, feeding on parasites and spreading cow manure, which improves soil health and reduces the need for chemical fertilizers.

Direct Sales: Polyface Farm sells directly to consumers and restaurants, emphasizing the importance of local food systems.

Outcomes: The farm has achieved substantial soil fertility improvements, high levels of biodiversity, and a profitable and sustainable business model, all while educating and inspiring other farmers through workshops and farm tours.

2. Rothamsted Research, England, UK

Background: Rothamsted Research in England is one of the oldest agricultural research institutions in the world, known for its long-term experiments in sustainable farming.

Practices Implemented:

Long-term Experimental Plots: Rothamsted has some of the longest-running experiments in agricultural science, providing invaluable data on soil health, crop yields, and sustainable farming practices.

Integrated Pest Management (IPM): The research includes developing and testing sustainable pest management systems, reducing the need for chemical pesticides.

Agroforestry and Biodiversity: They are also experimenting with agroforestry, integrating trees into farming landscapes to enhance biodiversity and ecosystem services.

Outcomes: Rothamsted's research has significantly contributed to sustainable agriculture practices worldwide, offering insights into soil health, crop sustainability, and environmental impacts over extended periods.

3. **Chido Govera's Mushroom Farming, Zimbabwe**

Background: Chido Govera, a Zimbabwean entrepreneur and farmer, has transformed lives through her sustainable mushroom farming initiative.

Practices Implemented:

Mushroom Cultivation on Waste: Chido teaches farmers, especially women and orphans, how to grow mushrooms using agricultural waste like coffee pulp, providing a source of food and income.

Community Empowerment: Her approach is community-centric, focusing on empowering marginalized groups through sustainable agriculture.

Education and Training: She offers workshops and training programs, spreading knowledge about sustainable and regenerative farming practices.

Outcomes: This initiative has not only provided food and income for many communities but also promoted sustainable use of resources and community resilience.

These case studies provide real-world evidence of how sustainable farming practices can lead to ecological health, community empowerment, and financial sustainability. Each example highlights different aspects of sustainable agriculture, from soil regeneration and biodiversity to community involvement and education. They serve as inspirational models for farmers globally, showing that sustainable practices can create thriving, resilient agricultural systems.

The transition to sustainable agriculture might seem daunting, but it is a rewarding journey. It's about striking a balance between economic viability and ecological and social responsibility. By adopting sustainable practices, farmers can ensure the long-term health and productivity of their land, contribute positively to their community and the environment, and build a resilient, prosperous agricultural business. The key is to start small, stay committed, and be open to learning and adapting along the way.

Chapter Seven — Monitoring and Evaluation

In the fertile plains that sweep across the heartland where I've farmed for over two decades, each sunrise offers a new lesson in the delicate balance of agriculture. Here, under the vast open skies, I've learned firsthand the critical importance of nurturing not just the crops we plant but the very soil that feeds them. This chapter is my attempt to distill decades of hands-on experience into insights that can empower small-scale farmers and avid home gardeners to optimize their yield and sustain their land.

Understanding Agricultural Health

Agricultural health is the cornerstone of any farming practice, whether you are cultivating a small vegetable garden in your backyard or managing hundreds of acres of crops. It encompasses the overall vitality of the farming ecosystem, including the quality of soil, the availability of water, the health of crops, and the balance of local biodiversity.

For us in the farming community, soil is not just dirt; it is a living, breathing entity that hosts a complex web of organisms. Its health dictates the nutritional value of the food we grow and, ultimately, the profitability of our endeavors. Therefore, assessing the health of your soil through regular testing for pH levels, nutrient content, and microbial activity is not just advisable; it's essential. This data provides the roadmap for amending soil deficiencies and selecting appropriate crops that will thrive in specific conditions.

Water management is another critical aspect of agricultural health. Efficient water use not only conserves this precious resource but also prevents issues like soil erosion, nutrient leaching, and uneven crop growth. Technologies such as drip irrigation and soil moisture sensors are becoming increasingly accessible and can significantly enhance water efficiency on a small farm.

Measuring, Monitoring, and Analyzing: Keys to Productivity

The ability to measure and monitor the various facets of farm health has revolutionized the way we farm today. Using simple tools like soil test kits and more advanced technology such as drones equipped with multispectral cameras, farmers can now get detailed insights into their land that were previously invisible to the naked eye.

For instance, drone technology allows us to monitor crop health on a large scale by capturing images that show variations in plant health, which can indicate pest attacks, disease presence, or nutritional deficiencies. This kind of monitoring leads to timely interventions, preventing minor issues from becoming farm-wide problems.

Data analysis plays a crucial role in modern agriculture. By analyzing data collected from the field, farmers can make informed decisions about crop rotation strategies, pest management, and fertilization plans. For example, by understanding the patterns of pest infestations over the years, farmers can predict and prevent future outbreaks, thereby reducing reliance on chemical pesticides.

Furthermore, the integration of geographic information systems (GIS) in agriculture helps in mapping and analyzing soil data and topography, aiding in precise planting and water management decisions. The use of these systems can significantly impact the efficiency of resource use and overall crop yield.

The Importance of a Proactive Approach

In my early years on the farm, I learned the hard way that reactive farming — responding to problems as they arise rather than anticipating them — often results in lower yields and higher costs. Adopting a proactive approach in measuring, monitoring, and analyzing agricultural health can lead to early detection of potential issues, allowing for interventions that can save crops and resources.

Moreover, this approach aids in sustainable farming practices. By understanding and working with the natural cycles and systems, we can enhance productivity while reducing environmental impact. Practices like cover cropping, reduced tillage, and organic pest control not only improve the health of the farm but also contribute to the ecological balance.

In conclusion, as farmers and stewards of the land, our task is not just to extract what we can from the earth but to enhance its health and ensure its productivity for generations to come. This is why a deep understanding of agricultural health and a commitment to its continuous measurement, monitoring, and analysis are not just beneficial but essential for every farmer aiming for successful agricultural practices.

The Five Principles of Soil Health

As I've cultivated various crops and observed the transformations of my own land over the years, I've come to recognize and respect the universal principles that govern soil health. These principles aren't merely guidelines; they are the bedrock upon which sustainable agriculture rests. Each principle addresses a fundamental aspect of the soil's ecosystem and, when implemented together, can dramatically improve the productivity and resilience of the land.

Minimize Disturbance

In traditional farming, plowing or tilling the soil is often seen as necessary to prepare the land for planting. However, my experience — and an increasing body of research — suggests that excessive tilling disrupts the soil structure, destroys microbial habitats, and leads to erosion and loss of nutrients. Minimizing disturbance preserves the soil architecture and allows earthworms and microbes to thrive, which in turn enhances soil aeration and nutrient cycling.

No-till farming, which involves planting crops directly into the residue of previous crops without tilling, has been a game changer on my farm. This practice reduces soil erosion and increases water infiltration, which is particularly beneficial during dry spells. Studies have shown that no-till farming can increase soil organic matter over time, which is crucial for sustaining soil fertility.

Maximize Soil Cover

Leaving soil bare is akin to leaving skin unprotected from the sun — it's vulnerable. Bare soil is prone to erosion by wind and water, and it can heat up more quickly, which can be detrimental to soil microbes. To protect the soil, I ensure it is always covered with either growing crops or mulches.

Cover crops, such as clover or rye, are planted during off-seasons when primary crops are not grown. These plants protect and enhance the soil by preventing erosion, improving soil structure, and adding organic matter when they decompose. Using organic mulches like straw or leaves also helps conserve moisture and suppress weeds, further reducing the need for chemical herbicides.

Diversify Plant Species

Monocropping — the practice of planting a single crop in the same field year after year — can deplete the soil of specific nutrients and increase vulnerability to pests and diseases. In contrast, diversifying plant species enhances soil biodiversity, which supports more robust plant health and soil structure.

Crop rotation and intercropping (growing different crops in close proximity) are practices I employ to maintain a diverse plant environment. This diversity helps in breaking pest and disease cycles and aids in the better utilization of nutrients, as different plants use and deposit different nutrients from and to the soil.

Maintain Living Roots Year-Round

Roots are not just the anchors of plants; they are vital to maintaining soil structure and health. Living roots exude sugars, amino acids, and organic acids, which feed soil microbes. These microbes, in turn, help make nutrients available to plants and bind soil particles together, improving structure.

To ensure that my soil always has living roots, I grow cover crops between commercial crop cycles. This practice ensures that there are always roots in the soil to support the microbial community and prevent nutrient leaching.

Integrate Livestock

Integrating livestock into crop production systems can have multifaceted benefits. Animals contribute to soil health through their manure, which enriches the soil with organic matter and nutrients. Additionally, their movement across the land can help break up compacted soil, which improves aeration and water infiltration.

On my farm, rotational grazing strategies are employed, where livestock are moved between different pastures. This prevents overgrazing and allows pastures time to recover, which is essential for maintaining the health of both the soil and the grasses.

Implementing these five principles of soil health has not only improved the productivity and sustainability of my farming practices but has also positioned my farm to be resilient against the challenges of climate change and shifting market demands. These principles are universal; whether you're a small-scale home gardener or a large-scale commercial farmer, their adoption can lead to healthier soil and more productive crops.

Yield Monitoring: The Link Between Soil Health and Crop Output

From the rich, earthy layers of soil we've discussed, the next natural step in our agricultural journey is understanding how the principles of soil health translate into tangible outcomes — namely, yield. Yield monitoring is a critical process that helps bridge the gap between the theoretical aspects of farming practices and their real-world impacts on crop production. In this section, we will delve into the comprehensive world of yield monitoring, explaining its purpose, exploring critical factors, discussing modern approaches, and examining mapping techniques.

Definition and Purpose

Yield monitoring refers to the process of quantifying the amount of agricultural produce harvested per unit area. This practice serves multiple purposes: it allows farmers like myself to assess the effectiveness of agronomic practices, provides insights into the health and productivity of the land, and helps in making informed decisions about future cultivation strategies.

On my farm, yield monitoring is not just about counting the bushels of corn or wheat at harvest; it's about understanding the relationship between various farming practices and their outcomes. It provides a feedback loop that helps refine techniques such as planting density, fertilization rates, and irrigation schedules. Essentially, yield monitoring helps to pinpoint what works well and what needs adjustment, ensuring that the land's productivity is maximized sustainably.

Critical Factors for Yield Determination

Geographic Location Data

The success of yield monitoring largely depends on accurate geographic location data. Knowing precisely where each portion of the yield comes from within a field allows for detailed analysis of spatial variability. For instance, GPS technology on my equipment enables the tracking of yield data to specific locations, revealing patterns related to soil types, sunlight exposure, and moisture availability.

Crop Flow Measurement

Measuring the rate at which crops are harvested (crop flow) is crucial for accurate yield monitoring. On my combine harvester, sensors track the amount of material passing through the machine. This data, when combined with the speed of the harvester and the area covered, provides a reliable measure of crop yield per unit area.

Moisture Content Measurement

Moisture content significantly affects yield measurements. Crops harvested at different moisture levels can weigh differently, which can distort yield calculations if not adjusted correctly. Therefore, integrating moisture sensors in the harvesting equipment ensures that yield data is corrected for moisture content, providing a more accurate yield estimate.

Approaches to Yield Monitoring

Sensor-Based Systems

Modern farms, including mine, increasingly rely on sensor-based systems integrated into harvesting machinery. These systems use various sensors to collect data on crop flow, moisture content, and combined location. The data are then processed to yield maps that visually depict the productivity across different field zones. This real-time data collection and analysis allow for immediate adjustments and long-term planning.

The primary significance of sensor-based systems lies in their ability to provide real-time data that can be visualized through yield maps. These maps are color-coded representations of the field, showing which parts are more productive and which are less so. This immediate feedback allows farmers like myself to make quick decisions on-the-fly, such as adjusting combine settings for optimal harvesting or planning immediate post-harvest activities. In the long run, this data helps in making informed decisions about fertilizer application, irrigation, and planting strategies to improve overall farm productivity and resource efficiency.

Optical Systems

Optical systems represent another sophisticated approach to yield monitoring. These systems use cameras and spectrometers to assess the quality and characteristics of the crop as it is harvested. By analyzing the light reflected from the crops, optical sensors can estimate parameters like grain quality, which is invaluable for crops destined for markets with strict quality requirements. Spectrometers go further to analyze the chemical properties of the crops by assessing the spectral signature, which is how different wavelengths of light are absorbed and reflected by the crops.

The use of optical systems is particularly significant for ensuring the quality of produce that meets market standards, especially for high-value crops where quality directly affects pricing. These systems provide a detailed, immediate analysis of grain quality during the harvesting process, which allows for real-time sorting — high-quality produce can be separated from lower quality. This sorting process is crucial for markets with stringent quality requirements and can significantly enhance profitability through premium pricing.

Mapping Techniques

Use of GIS and Remote Sensing

Geographic Information Systems (GIS) and remote sensing technologies are vital tools in yield monitoring. They allow for the integration and analysis of data collected from various sources, including yield monitors, soil health assessments, and satellite images. On my farm, GIS is used to create detailed yield maps that show variations across the field, which can be correlated with data on soil health, topography, and crop management practices.

The integration of GIS and remote sensing is transformative for precision agriculture. By creating detailed maps that show variations in yield along with corresponding data on soil conditions and other environmental factors, farmers can pinpoint specific areas that require attention or adjustment in their management practices. For instance, if certain zones consistently show lower yields, a farmer can investigate further by checking soil health indicators and adjusting management practices accordingly, such as altering fertilizer types or amounts, adjusting irrigation schedules, or planning soil conservation measures.

Data Integration and Analysis

The real power of yield monitoring lies in the integration and analysis of the collected data. By combining yield data with soil health metrics, weather information, and management practices, we can create comprehensive models that predict and enhance farm productivity. Advanced data analytics tools allow me to understand complex relationships and make informed decisions that align closely with sustainable farming objectives.

For instance, understanding how certain practices like crop rotation or cover cropping influence yield outcomes enables farmers to tailor their strategies to meet both economic and environmental goals. The analysis can reveal patterns and insights that are not immediately obvious, guiding strategic decisions that lead to improved crop performance and resource use efficiency. This holistic approach ensures that every aspect of farm management is aligned toward achieving maximum productivity and sustainability.

Linking yield monitoring back to soil health, the principles discussed in the previous section directly influence the data gathered through these monitoring techniques. Practices that promote soil health, such as minimizing soil disturbance and maintaining organic cover, not only enhance the quality of the soil but also reflect positively on yield outputs. This symbiotic relationship underscores the importance of a holistic approach to farming, where every practice is interlinked and aimed at achieving optimal productivity and sustainability.

Financial Tracking and Analysis in Agriculture

After years spent observing the seasonal ebbs and flows of the agricultural cycle, I've come to recognize that successful farming is as much about financial acumen as it is about agronomic expertise. Financial tracking and analysis provide the framework for understanding the economic impacts of farming decisions, offering insights that are crucial for sustaining and growing a farming enterprise. This section will explore the essentials of farm financial analysis, delve into common methodologies, and discuss the prevalent financial challenges that farmers face.

Purpose and Benefits

Financial analysis in farming serves to illuminate the economic health and viability of a farming operation. It involves systematically reviewing financial statements, tracking cash flows, and analyzing investment returns to make informed decisions. The primary benefits of conducting regular financial analysis include:

Improved Financial Planning: Understanding financial trends helps in budgeting and forecasting, enabling farmers to plan for seasonal expenditures and potential expansions.

Risk Management: By regularly assessing financial health, farmers can identify potential financial risks early, such as cash flow shortages or over-leveraging, and take preventive measures.

Enhanced Profitability: Detailed financial analysis helps pinpoint areas where costs can be reduced and yields can be maximized, directly contributing to enhanced profitability.

In my own farming operation, routine financial analysis has been instrumental in navigating the uncertainties of agricultural production, aiding in decision-making processes from purchasing new equipment to selecting crops for the coming seasons.

Methods of Agricultural Financial Analysis

Cash Flow Analysis

Cash flow analysis is fundamental in agriculture, where income is often seasonal and expenses can be high. It involves recording all cash inflows and outflows within a given period, allowing farmers to understand their liquidity position — essentially, the availability of cash to cover obligations.

1. **Record Keeping:** I maintain detailed records of all cash receipts and expenditures. This includes sales of crops and livestock, any direct payments from agricultural programs, operational expenses like seed and fertilizer purchases, labor costs, and machinery maintenance.
2. **Categorization:** I categorize cash flows into operating, investing, and financing activities. Operating activities cover the day-to-day expenses and income, investing activities include the purchase or sale of long-term assets like equipment and land, and financing activities encompass loans and other forms of capital inflow.
3. **Projection:** Based on historical data and future expectations (e.g., market price and yield forecasts), I project future cash flows. This involves estimating when major expenses will occur and forecasting

income from crop sales, taking into account seasonal patterns and market conditions.
4. **Analysis:** I analyze these projections to identify periods of potential cash shortages or surpluses. This allows me to plan for necessary financial activities, such as arranging for a line of credit or planning capital investments during surplus periods.
5. **Monitoring:** Regular monitoring and updating of cash flow projections are crucial, especially as real-time market and environmental conditions can alter financial landscapes quickly. Adjustments are made as needed to stay aligned with both short-term needs and long-term financial goals.

Investment and Return Analysis

Investment analysis involves evaluating the costs and benefits of major purchases and projects, such as acquiring new land or investing in advanced irrigation systems. Return on investment (ROI) calculations help determine whether these investments are likely to be profitable.

For example, before integrating a new tractor into my fleet, I analyze the expected increase in productivity against the cost of the tractor, including financing costs and depreciation. This approach ensures that each major investment contributes positively to the farm's overall financial health.

1. **Identifying Costs:** All potential costs associated with the investment are identified. This includes the initial outlay, ongoing operational costs, maintenance, and

any financing costs if the investment is funded through borrowing.
2. **Estimating Returns:** Returns are estimated based on additional revenue or cost savings the investment is expected to generate. For example, a new tractor might increase planting efficiency, reducing labor costs and increasing the potential planting area.
3. **Time Frame:** I consider the time frame over which the returns will be realized. Agricultural investments often have a long-term horizon, so it's important to calculate the return on investment over the expected life of the asset.
4. **Calculating ROI:** The return on investment (ROI) is calculated by comparing the total returns to the total costs over the investment period. This helps in determining the break-even point and overall profitability of the investment.
5. **Risk Assessment:** I assess the risks associated with the investment, such as potential market changes or unexpected increases in operational costs, and consider these in the final decision-making process.

Common Financial Challenges in Agriculture

Market Volatility

Agricultural markets are notoriously volatile, influenced by a myriad of factors, including weather conditions, global market trends, and geopolitical events. Prices for crops and livestock can fluctuate widely, making financial planning challenging. Strategies such as futures contracts and crop insurance can mitigate some of these risks, but they require careful financial analysis and market insight.

Cost Management

Managing costs is crucial for maintaining profitability in farming. Variable costs such as fuel, fertilizers, and seeds, as well as fixed costs like land payments and equipment depreciation, must be carefully managed. Regular financial analysis helps identify areas where efficiencies can be gained, such as optimizing input use or renegotiating supplier contracts.

Access to Capital

Access to capital is a critical issue for many farmers, especially those expanding operations or recovering from poor seasons. Financial institutions often view agriculture as a high-risk industry due to its dependency on uncontrollable factors like weather. Building a strong financial record through meticulous tracking and analysis can improve access to loans and credit, which is essential for growth and sustainability.

In conclusion, financial tracking and analysis are not merely administrative tasks; they are integral to the strategic management and long-term success of a farming operation. By understanding and implementing robust financial analysis techniques, farmers can navigate the complexities of agricultural economics, optimize their operations, and secure their financial future against the unpredictable nature of farming.

Effective cost management is essential for maintaining farm profitability. Here's how I manage costs:

1. **Budgeting:** I create detailed budgets that outline expected costs and income across different farm activities. This helps in tracking actual expenses against projections and identifying variances that need addressing.
2. **Cost Tracking:** I track costs continuously, using accounting software tailored to agricultural needs. This allows for real-time monitoring and helps in making quick adjustments to farm operations.
3. **Benchmarking:** By comparing my costs with industry benchmarks, I identify areas where the farm is not operating efficiently. This could lead to changes in suppliers, negotiation for better rates, or investment in more efficient technologies.
4. **Regular Reviews:** I conduct regular reviews of all farm costs, looking for trends or changes that could indicate problems or opportunities for savings. This includes a close look at variable costs that can fluctuate significantly, such as energy prices or input costs.

In conclusion, the continuous monitoring and evaluation of agricultural practices are not merely routine tasks but essential components of successful farming. Over two decades of hands-on experience have taught me that understanding and improving the health of our agricultural systems is key to sustaining productivity. Techniques like yield monitoring and sophisticated data analysis enable us to make informed decisions that optimize resource use and enhance crop output. These efforts, coupled with a proactive approach to managing soil health and water use, help ensure that our farming practices are both sustainable and productive. As we pass on these insights and techniques, we empower the next generation of farmers and gardeners to achieve greater success and sustainability, preserving the vitality of our lands for future generations.

Chapter Eight — Modern Agricultural Challenges and Case Studies

As a farmer with years tending to the earth under my boots, I've watched as the landscape of agriculture has shifted under the pressures of modern demands and global challenges. Farming isn't just about planting seeds and harvesting crops; it's about understanding and navigating the complex web of environmental, economic, and technological factors that impact how we grow our food.

The challenges we face today are as varied as they are critical. Water scarcity, for instance, is becoming increasingly severe. According to the United Nations, agriculture consumes about 70% of the global freshwater supply, yet we're seeing sources diminish faster than they can be replenished. Soil degradation is another critical issue; the FAO reports that approximately 33% of the Earth's soils are already degraded, and with continuing practices that strip soil health, this figure is only expected to rise. Moreover, the specter of climate change looms large, altering weather patterns and making crop cultivation more unpredictable than ever.

But it's not just natural resources that are strained. The agricultural sector also faces economic pressures from fluctuating market demands, trade policies, and a need to adapt to sustainable practices that may require upfront investment. As the population grows, the demand for farmers to increase productivity without compromising the environment intensifies.

The Role of Real-Time Case Studies

In this ever-evolving scenario, real-time case studies become invaluable. They're not just academic exercises; they're practical, real-world examples of how farmers are adapting to challenges today. These case studies provide us with a window into the effectiveness of different approaches in various contexts. For instance, a recent study published by the International Water Management Institute highlighted how farmers in semi-arid regions of India have successfully adopted micro-irrigation systems to dramatically reduce water usage while boosting crop yields by up to 50%.

Such insights are crucial for us, especially small-scale farmers and home gardeners, as they offer tested solutions that can be tailored to our unique needs and conditions. By learning from the successes and failures of others, we can adopt practices that are not only sustainable but also enhance our productivity and profitability.

In the following sections, we'll dive deeper into specific challenges and explore how real farmers around the globe are harnessing innovation and tradition to turn adversity into opportunity. Whether it's through advanced technology or revitalizing ancient practices, there's much to learn and even more to implement.

Challenge One — Water Scarcity and Irrigation Issues

Water scarcity is among the most pressing issues facing agriculture today. As farmers, we depend on reliable water sources not just for the survival of our crops but for the very sustenance of our communities. Globally, this challenge is exacerbated by factors such as climate change, population growth, and increased urbanization, all of which strain our natural water reserves. The United Nations has projected that by 2025, two-thirds of the world's population may face water shortages, and with agriculture consuming about 70% of global freshwater, the sector is at a critical juncture.

The impact of water scarcity is not uniformly distributed; it disproportionately affects those in arid and semi-arid regions where rainfall is scarce and evaporation rates are high. However, even in regions with substantial rainfall, inefficient water use and management can lead to unsustainable agricultural practices. This necessitates an urgent need to adopt more efficient irrigation techniques that can reduce wastage and maximize water usage efficiency.

Case Study: Implementation of Smart Irrigation Systems in Israel

Israel, a country characterized by its dry climate and limited water resources, has been at the forefront of tackling water scarcity through technological innovation. Over the decades, Israeli farmers have turned adversity into an advantage by implementing advanced irrigation techniques, most notably smart irrigation systems.

Technology Optimization of Water Use

Smart irrigation technology in Israel primarily revolves around drip irrigation systems and the integration of real-time data analytics to optimize water use. Drip irrigation delivers water directly to the plant's roots through a network of valves, pipes, and emitters, minimizing evaporation and runoff. This method is highly efficient, reducing water usage by up to 60% compared to traditional flood irrigation methods.

Moreover, these systems are often equipped with sensors that monitor soil moisture levels, weather conditions, and even plant health. This data is fed into a central system that uses algorithms to calculate the optimal watering schedule and amount. By automating irrigation, farmers can ensure that crops receive the precise amount of water at the right time, further enhancing water use efficiency.

Results and Ongoing Impact on Agricultural Efficiency

The results of implementing these smart irrigation systems in Israel have been profound. According to research from the Israeli Ministry of Agriculture, the introduction of smart irrigation has led to a reduction in water usage by up to 50% across various crops. Furthermore, crop yields have increased significantly due to the more targeted and efficient watering practices, showcasing a perfect example of how technological innovation can lead to more sustainable farming practices.

The ongoing impact of these systems extends beyond just water savings and increased agricultural productivity. By reducing the amount of water needed for irrigation, Israel has been able to alleviate pressure on its limited freshwater resources, contributing to greater environmental sustainability. Additionally, the success of these systems has spurred similar adaptations in other parts of the world, promoting global food security and the sustainability of water resources.

For small-scale farmers and home gardeners, the Israeli case presents a valuable lesson in the potential of technology to address critical issues like water scarcity. While the initial setup and technology might be an investment, the long-term benefits of reduced water costs and higher crop productivity can make this a viable solution for those facing similar challenges.

Challenge Two — Soil Degradation and Sustainability

Soil is the foundation of agriculture, a living resource essential for the production of food and the sustenance of our ecosystems. Yet, this critical asset is under threat from soil degradation — a process that diminishes the soil's ability to function effectively. Across the globe, practices such as overcultivation, chemical overuse, and neglect of soil health management are accelerating the degradation of soils, thereby reducing the land's agricultural productivity and resilience to environmental changes.

Overview of Soil Health Issues and Sustainability Concerns

Soil degradation takes many forms, including erosion, salinization, compaction, and chemical pollution. These processes strip the soil of nutrients, reduce its organic matter, and impair its structure and water retention capacity. According to the Food and Agriculture Organization (FAO), about one-third of the world's soil is degraded, and without intervention, this could worsen, significantly impacting food security and sustainability.

Sustainability concerns are paramount because soil is not a resource that can be readily replaced. Once degraded, the restoration of soil health can take decades, if not longer, making its conservation vital for future generations. Sustainable soil management is essential not just for crop productivity but for water management, carbon sequestration, and biodiversity — all of which contribute to ecological stability.

Case Study: Regenerative Agriculture Practices in Brazil

Brazil, a country with a vast agricultural footprint, has been facing significant challenges with soil degradation, particularly in regions with intensive agricultural activities. However, it has also become a pioneer in adopting regenerative agriculture practices aimed at restoring soil health and enhancing crop productivity.

Explanation of Techniques Used

Regenerative agriculture in Brazil focuses on techniques that rebuild soil organic matter and restore degraded soil biodiversity. Key practices include:

Crop Rotation: This involves growing a variety of crops in succession on the same land to improve soil structure and reduce soil erosion. Rotating crops helps in breaking cycles of pests and diseases and can improve soil fertility by utilizing plants that fix nitrogen in the soil.

Cover Cropping: Brazilian farmers use cover crops to protect and enrich the soil during times when primary crops are not sown. Cover crops such as vetch, clover, and rye are planted to cover the soil, which helps prevent erosion, suppress weeds, and enhance soil moisture levels. These plants also add organic matter to the soil through their roots and decaying vegetation, which improves soil structure and fertility.

Assessment of Improvements in Soil Health and Crop Yields

The adoption of these practices has led to notable improvements in soil health across various regions of Brazil. Studies coordinated by the FAO have shown that areas practicing regenerative techniques have seen increases in soil organic matter, which significantly enhances water retention and nutrient availability. This, in turn, has led to higher crop yields and greater resilience to drought and heavy rains.

Moreover, the economic benefits are clear: farmers report lower costs on inputs like fertilizers and pesticides and higher outputs due to improved crop health and yields. These practices not only enhance the sustainability of farms but also contribute to larger environmental goals such as carbon sequestration, crucial for mitigating climate change.

In conclusion, Brazil's experience with regenerative agriculture highlights the transformative potential of adopting sustainable practices in reversing soil degradation and ensuring the long-term viability of farming. For small-scale farmers and home gardeners, implementing similar techniques can be a pathway to more productive and sustainable agricultural systems, proving that good soil health is the bedrock of successful farming.

Challenge Three — Impact of Climate Change on Crop Production

As an experienced farmer, I've felt the pressing impacts of climate change first-hand. It's an undeniable force altering the way we approach the very basics of crop production. The shifting climate affects agriculture through increased temperatures, altered precipitation patterns, and more frequent extreme weather events like droughts and floods. These changes not only threaten crop viability but also challenge farmers to adapt swiftly to maintain productivity.

How Changing Climates Affect Agriculture

Climate change impacts agriculture in several direct and indirect ways. Directly, changes in temperature and precipitation can affect crop growth cycles, potentially leading to reduced yields. For instance, increased temperatures can accelerate crop maturation, reducing the growing period and thus decreasing yield. Indirectly, climate change influences the prevalence of pests and diseases, alters soil moisture and nutrient levels, and can even transform agricultural landscapes through changes in water availability and soil erosion.

Moreover, the increasing unpredictability of weather patterns makes planning and management increasingly challenging for farmers. The need for adaptive strategies and innovative farming techniques has never been more critical.

Case Study: Drought-Resistant Crops in Australia

In response to these challenges, Australia has been at the forefront of developing and deploying drought-resistant crops through advanced genetic engineering and breeding programs.

This initiative is crucial for Australian agriculture, as the continent frequently faces severe drought conditions exacerbated by climate change.

Overview of Genetic Engineering and Breeding Programs

Australian scientists and agronomists have been working collaboratively on breeding programs that focus on enhancing the genetic traits of crops to withstand arid conditions. These programs utilize both traditional breeding techniques and modern biotechnology to develop plant varieties that can maintain productivity and quality despite limited water availability.

One approach has been to identify and incorporate genes that help plants manage water stress better. These genes enable plants to adjust their physiological processes, such as closing their stomata to reduce water loss and altering root structures to optimize water uptake.

Crop Resilience in Australian Farms

The results from fields across Australia have been promising. According to data from the Australian Bureau of Agricultural and Resource Economics and Sciences, the implementation of drought-resistant varieties has led to a noticeable improvement in crop resilience. Farmers who have adopted these new varieties report that their crops can survive longer during dry spells and recover more quickly after drought conditions ease.

Moreover, the adoption of these crops has not only stabilized yields under challenging conditions but has also allowed farmers to continue cultivating lands that might otherwise have been left fallow. This adaptability is crucial for maintaining food supply chains and supporting rural economies in the face of climate variability.

These drought-resistant crops are a testament to the power of science and innovation in agriculture. They offer a practical solution to one of the most pressing challenges posed by climate change, providing a lifeline for farmers in drought-prone regions.

Successful Implementation Stories

Case Study One — Advanced Greenhouse Techniques in the Netherlands

The Netherlands, a small country with a significant impact on global agriculture, has become synonymous with innovation in greenhouse farming. Dutch farmers and scientists have developed some of the most advanced greenhouse technologies in the world, turning their small nation into a powerhouse of agricultural productivity. These technologies not only maximize crop yields but also set benchmarks in sustainability and efficiency.

The innovative Dutch greenhouse designs focus on optimizing every element of the plant growth environment. One of the key innovations is the use of diffuse glass with anti-reflective coating, which scatters sunlight more evenly within the greenhouse, ensuring that light penetrates deeper into the lower parts of the plants. This technology maximizes natural sunlight usage, reducing the need for artificial lighting and thereby saving energy.

Temperature control is another area where Dutch greenhouses excel. They employ a variety of techniques to manage internal temperatures, including high-tech shading systems and energy screens that can open or close automatically to either retain or reflect heat. This precision allows for the cultivation of crops that are traditionally difficult to grow in the temperate Dutch climate.

Moreover, these greenhouses often incorporate closed water systems that not only recycle water but also capture and reuse nutrient runoff. Advanced sensors monitor plant conditions and soil moisture levels, ensuring that water and nutrients are precisely delivered to where they're needed most, minimizing waste and reducing environmental impact.

Impact on Productivity and Sustainability

The results of implementing these technologies are staggering. According to the Dutch Horticulture Innovation Council, these greenhouses can produce yields up to 20 times higher per hectare than traditional farming methods. For example, a typical Dutch greenhouse can produce around 70 kilograms of tomatoes per square meter, compared to 3-4 kilograms per square meter in an open field in a similar climate.

Sustainability metrics are equally impressive. These greenhouses use up to 90% less water than traditional agriculture due to their recycling systems. Energy efficiency is also a hallmark of the Dutch model; for instance, new geothermal energy projects have reduced the dependency on natural gas, cutting carbon emissions by up to 30% in some operations.

Furthermore, the integration of renewable energy sources, like solar panels on greenhouse roofs, has allowed several farms to operate nearly energy-neutral. This level of innovation in energy efficiency and waste reduction exemplifies the potential for sustainable agriculture practices to mitigate the broader impacts of farming on the environment.

The success of Dutch greenhouse technology has not only revolutionized farming in the Netherlands but also serves as a model for countries worldwide, demonstrating how technology can help overcome natural resource limitations and climate challenges. This case study is a beacon for small-scale farmers and home gardeners, showing that with the right technology and innovative practices, it is possible to significantly enhance both productivity and sustainability in agriculture.

Case Study Two — Precision Farming Technologies in the USA

In the vast and varied landscapes of the United States, precision farming technologies have transformed agricultural practices, ushering in a new era of efficiency and data-driven decision-making. This approach to farming uses advanced technologies such as artificial intelligence (AI) and drones to enhance crop monitoring and management, aiming to maximize yields while minimizing environmental impacts.

Discussion on the Use of AI and Drones for Crop Monitoring and Management

Precision farming in the U.S. leverages AI to analyze data collected from various sources, including satellites, drones, and ground sensors. This data might include information on soil conditions, crop health, weather patterns, and pest infestations.

AI algorithms process this information to provide actionable insights, such as identifying the optimal times for planting, watering, or applying fertilizers and pesticides.

Drones play a crucial role in this technological ecosystem. Equipped with high-resolution cameras and other sensors, drones fly over fields to collect detailed images and data that are not easily accessible at ground level. These aerial devices can cover large areas quickly, providing real-time insights that help farmers assess crop health, monitor growth, and even detect weed or pest issues. This bird's-eye view allows for precise intervention, reducing the wastage of inputs like water, fertilizers, and pesticides.

The adoption of precision farming technologies across the United States has been bolstered by support from institutions like the USDA National Institute of Food and Agriculture, which funds research and development in this field. This support has facilitated a wide-ranging adoption of precision agriculture tools, leading to significant improvements in farm operations.

For instance, the application of these technologies has led to more precise planting, which improves seed placement accuracy and optimizes spacing. This precision enhances germination rates and plant growth, ultimately boosting crop yields. Moreover, precise application of inputs helps reduce costs and decrease the environmental impact of farming. Farmers report reductions in chemical use by up to 40%, which not only cuts costs but also lessens soil and water contamination.

The use of these technologies also contributes to sustainability by enabling better water management. Through precise irrigation techniques that account for real-time soil moisture levels and weather forecasts, water usage can be optimized, preserving this valuable resource.

Furthermore, the data-driven nature of precision farming helps in making long-term decisions about crop rotation and land management, improving soil health and sustainability of the land over time. This holistic approach to farm management supports a more sustainable agricultural sector that can adapt to and mitigate the effects of climate change.

The implementation of precision farming technologies in the USA exemplifies how technological innovation can lead to revolutionary changes in agricultural practices. These technologies not only enhance the efficiency and productivity of farms but also play a critical role in promoting environmental sustainability. As small-scale farmers and home gardeners, adopting elements of precision agriculture, even on a smaller scale, can provide significant benefits, making agriculture smarter, more sustainable, and more productive.

Lessons Learned from Other Small Farms: Historical Perspectives

The agricultural history of small farms is rich with examples of adaptive strategies and innovative practices that have allowed these enterprises to thrive despite numerous challenges. This overview will delve into the historical approaches small farms across Europe have implemented to navigate environmental, economic, and social hurdles. These strategies often combine traditional knowledge with small-scale adaptability, offering valuable lessons for today's agricultural challenges.

Mixed Farming Techniques in Small European Farms

Mixed farming, a method where crops and livestock are raised together on the same land, has been a cornerstone of European agriculture for centuries. This technique maximizes resource use efficiently, cycling nutrients between animals and crops, which enhances soil fertility and reduces dependence on chemical fertilizers. A prime example can be found in the rotation systems used in the 18th century, such as the Norfolk four-course system, which alternated crops like wheat, turnips, barley, and clover. This rotation not only improved soil structure and fertility but also supported varied livestock, contributing to a self-sustaining farm ecosystem.

Over the decades, these mixed farming techniques have evolved in response to changing agricultural demands and advancements in agricultural science. The introduction of mechanization in the early 20th century, for instance, transformed traditional practices, increasing the scale and efficiency of crop production. However, the core principles of mixed farming — particularly the integration of crops and livestock — have seen a resurgence in popularity as modern farms seek sustainable and eco-friendly farming solutions.

Today's small farms face a myriad of challenges, from the pressures of global competition to the threats posed by climate change. The historical model of mixed farming offers several lessons that are highly relevant in addressing these issues:

1. **Resource Efficiency:** By integrating crop and livestock production, farms can achieve greater resource efficiency, reduce waste, and minimize their environmental footprint.
2. **Biodiversity:** Mixed farming supports biodiversity at the micro-level, promoting a variety of crops and livestock breeds, which can be crucial for resilience in the face of climate variability.
3. **Economic Sustainability:** Diversification in mixed farming provides multiple streams of income, buffering small farms against market fluctuations and crop failures.

In conclusion, the historical strategies employed by small farms in Europe, particularly mixed farming techniques, provide enduring lessons that can be adapted to modern agricultural challenges. By revisiting and revitalizing these traditional practices, today's farmers can address sustainability in agriculture more effectively, ensuring food security and economic stability in rural communities. As these methods continue to evolve, they remind us of the enduring wisdom embedded in historical agricultural practices, reinforcing the need for a balanced harmony between tradition and innovation.

Cropping System Research

Recent advancements in cropping system research have significantly contributed to sustainable agriculture by focusing on innovations that enhance productivity while minimizing environmental impact. One of the most crucial areas of this research is the development and implementation of Integrated Pest Management (IPM) systems. IPM is a holistic approach that utilizes multiple agricultural practices aimed at controlling pest populations in an environmentally and economically sustainable way. This method combines biological, cultural, physical, and chemical tools in a coordinated way to manage pest and disease problems while minimizing risks to human health and the environment.

Integrated Pest Management (IPM) Systems

Integrated Pest Management (IPM) strategies have evolved considerably due to continuous research and technological innovations. Recent developments include the use of pheromone traps for monitoring pest populations, genetically modified crops that are resistant to specific pests, and biological control agents that target and suppress pest populations naturally. Additionally, advancements in information technology, such as AI and data analytics, have led to the development of precision agriculture tools that can predict pest outbreaks and optimize the timing and application of pest control measures.

These practical applications of IPM have been shown to reduce the reliance on chemical pesticides, lower production costs, and increase crop yields. Furthermore, IPM practices contribute to the long-term sustainability of farming ecosystems by preserving beneficial insect populations and reducing the risk of pests developing resistance to control methods.

Case Study on Successful IPM Implementation in Kenya

A notable example of successful IPM implementation can be found in Kenya, where smallholder farmers have adopted IPM strategies to combat pests in maize cultivation, a staple crop in the region. This case study, facilitated by the International Crops

Research Institute for the Semi-Arid Tropics (ICRISAT), illustrates the effectiveness of IPM in improving crop productivity and sustainability.

Kenyan farmers faced significant challenges from the Fall Armyworm, an invasive pest that threatened maize across sub-Saharan Africa. Through the ICRISAT initiative, researchers introduced a combination of biological control agents, specifically parasitoids and entomopathogenic fungi. They educated farmers on crop rotation and intercropping with legumes to disrupt the pest's life cycle. Additionally, pheromone traps were distributed to help monitor pest populations more effectively.

The results were profound. The IPM program led to a substantial decrease in pesticide use, with a reported reduction of up to 50% in some areas, while maize yields increased by approximately 20%. The success of this program not only provided a sustainable solution to pest management but also served as a model for other regions facing similar challenges.

In conclusion, the ongoing research in cropping system strategies, particularly in the area of Integrated Pest Management, offers promising solutions for sustainable agriculture. The success of IPM in Kenya exemplifies how blending traditional knowledge with modern scientific innovations can lead to significant advancements in agricultural sustainability, providing a roadmap for other regions and crops worldwide.

The challenges facing modern agriculture are multifaceted, from water scarcity and soil degradation to the disruptive impacts of climate change. However, real-world case studies showcase how farmers around the globe are innovating and adapting, leveraging both cutting-edge technologies and reviving traditional practices. Whether it's implementing smart irrigation systems in Israel, adopting regenerative techniques in Brazil, developing drought-resistant crops in Australia, or integrating precision farming tools in the USA, these success stories demonstrate the power of ingenuity and collaboration in ensuring sustainable food production. As we look ahead, continued research into areas like integrated pest management and efficient cropping systems will be vital. By learning from these pioneering efforts and building on ancestral wisdom, the agricultural community can pave the way for a more resilient, productive, and environmentally conscious future.

Chapter Nine — Tools and Resources

Cultivating a thriving crop is fundamental to the livelihoods of small-scale farmers and home gardeners like you and me. It's more than just a source of food and income — it's a way to contribute to environmental sustainability, food security, and the well-being of our communities. Can you believe that according to the Food and Agriculture Organization (FAO), small-scale farmers produce over 70% of the world's food supply? That's an incredible statistic that highlights our crucial role in feeding the global population.

But successful crop cultivation isn't just about the numbers — it's about the sense of accomplishment and self-sufficiency that comes with nurturing your own crops. It's about preserving cultural traditions and fostering a resilient community. When we cultivate our crops with care and sustainable practices, we're not only ensuring a bountiful harvest but also promoting biodiversity, soil health, and resource conservation for generations to come.

Factors Influencing Crop Success

Now, we all know that achieving a successful crop isn't as simple as planting a few seeds and waiting for the magic to happen. It's a complex process influenced by various factors, and understanding these factors is key to maximizing your crop yields and quality.

Let's start with the foundation – soil health. Our soil is the lifeblood of our plants, providing essential nutrients, moisture, and structure for growth. By implementing proper soil management techniques like crop rotation, cover cropping, and incorporating organic matter, we can significantly improve soil fertility and structure, giving our crops the best possible start.

Next, we have to consider the climate conditions. Temperature, precipitation, and sunlight all play a vital role in our crops' development. That's why selecting crop varieties that are well-suited to our local climate and implementing strategies to mitigate adverse weather conditions, like irrigation or shade structures, can make all the difference in crop success.

But even with the perfect soil and climate conditions, our crops can still face challenges from pesky pests and diseases. That's where effective pest and disease management comes into play. By using Integrated Pest Management (IPM) strategies that combine cultural, biological, and judicious chemical control methods, we can minimize pest damage while reducing our environmental impact.

And let's not forget about cultivation techniques like proper planting, spacing, and pruning. These seemingly small details can have a big impact on plant growth and yield potential. Plus, having access to quality seeds or seedlings and appropriate tools and equipment can give us a significant advantage in our crop cultivation journey.

By understanding and addressing these factors, we can increase our chances of achieving a bountiful and sustainable harvest, contributing to our food security, economic well-being, and environmental stewardship. It's a rewarding journey and one that we can navigate together.

Essential Resources and Tools

As small-scale farmers and home gardeners, we know that having the right resources and tools can make all the difference in our crop cultivation efforts. These resources provide invaluable knowledge, guidance, and practical support throughout the cultivation process, empowering us to make informed decisions and implement best practices.

Recommended Reading and Literature

Knowledge is power, and accessing reliable and up-to-date information is crucial for making informed decisions and implementing best practices in crop cultivation. Fortunately, there's a wealth of reading materials and literature sources available to us as resources.

Books and Journals

Let's start with the classics — books and journals remain essential sources of comprehensive and in-depth knowledge on various aspects of crop cultivation. Some highly recommended titles that have become go-to resources for many farmers and gardeners include:

The New Organic Grower **by Eliot Coleman:** This comprehensive guide covers a wide range of topics, from soil management to crop selection, and emphasizes sustainable and organic farming practices that are kinder to our planet.

The Vegetable Gardener's Bible **by Edward C. Smith:** A true bible for home gardeners, this book covers everything from site selection and soil preparation to harvesting and storage, making it an invaluable companion for our gardening journey.

*The Farmer's Almanac***:** Published annually, this almanac provides valuable information on planting dates, weather forecasts, and gardening tips tailored to specific regions, helping us plan and prepare for the growing season ahead.

HortScience and *Journal of Vegetable Crop Production*: For those seeking a more scientific perspective, these peer-reviewed journals offer cutting-edge research and insights into various aspects of horticulture and vegetable crop production.

Online Resources and Websites

In the digital age, the internet has become a vast repository of agricultural information, offering a wealth of resources and tools at our fingertips. Some notable online resources include:

- **University and Extension Service Websites:** Many universities and agricultural extension services provide free online resources, including fact sheets, guides, and educational videos on various crop cultivation topics, making knowledge accessible to all.
- **Online Forums and Communities:** Platforms like GardenWeb, Permies, and GrowingForMarket allow us to connect with fellow farmers and gardeners, share experiences, and seek advice from experienced peers, fostering a sense of community and collaboration.
- **Mobile Apps:** Apps like Plantix, GrowVeg, and Farmer's Almanac offer convenient crop

identification, planting calendars, weather data, and pest management information tailored to our specific locations, putting valuable knowledge right in our pockets.
- **Online Courses and Webinars:** Organizations like the Sustainable Agriculture Research and Education (SARE) program and eXtension offer free online courses, webinars, and educational materials on sustainable farming practices, providing opportunities for continuous learning and skill development.

Essential Tools and Equipment

While knowledge is essential, having the right tools and equipment is equally crucial for efficient and effective crop cultivation. The specific tools required may vary depending on the scale of our operations and the crops we're growing, but some essential tools and equipment include:

Hand Tools

For small-scale operations and home gardens, hand tools are our trusted companions. These tools include spades, shovels, and forks for digging, turning soil, and moving materials; hoes and cultivators for weeding, aerating soil, and creating furrows for planting; pruning shears and loppers for maintaining healthy plant growth; and gardening gloves and knee pads to protect our hard-working hands and knees during manual labor.

Machinery and Implements

While hand tools are suitable for small-scale operations, machinery and implements can significantly increase efficiency and productivity for larger operations. Some essential machinery and implements include tillers and cultivators for soil preparation, weed control, and crop maintenance; seeders and planters for precise and efficient seed planting; irrigation equipment like drip irrigation systems, sprinklers, and hoses for consistent water distribution and conservation; and harvest aids like harvesters, wagons, and crates for efficient crop harvesting and transportation.

Irrigation Systems

Proper irrigation is vital for ensuring adequate water supply to our crops, particularly in regions with irregular or insufficient rainfall. Several irrigation systems are available, each with its advantages and suitability for different scales of operation and crop types:

- **Drip Irrigation:** This water-efficient system delivers water directly to the root zone, minimizing water loss through evaporation and runoff. It's well-suited for row crops, orchards, and small-scale operations.
- **Sprinkler Systems:** Suitable for larger areas, sprinkler systems can distribute water evenly over crops and landscapes. Overhead sprinklers, impact

sprinklers, and traveling sprinklers are common types used in agriculture.
- **Flood or Furrow Irrigation:** This traditional method involves directing water through furrows or channels between crop rows and is often used for larger-scale operations and crops like rice, cotton, and corn.
- **Rain Barrels and Catchment Systems:** For home gardens and small-scale operations, collecting and storing rainwater can supplement irrigation needs and promote water conservation, making the most of nature's bounty.

Regardless of the irrigation system we choose, proper installation, maintenance, and efficient water management are essential for optimal crop growth and water conservation, ensuring that our efforts are sustainable and respectful of this precious resource.

Investing in the appropriate resources, tools, and equipment can significantly contribute to successful crop cultivation for small-scale farmers and home gardeners like us. By utilizing reliable information sources, efficient tools, and suitable irrigation systems, we can maximize our crop yields, optimize resource utilization, and promote sustainable farming practices that benefit both our communities and our planet.

Farming Practices and Techniques

Successful crop cultivation is a labor of love, and it relies heavily on implementing appropriate farming practices and techniques tailored to our specific crops and local conditions. From soil preparation to post-harvest handling, each step plays a crucial role in maximizing yields, ensuring crop quality, and promoting sustainable farming methods that respect and nurture our land.

Soil Preparation and Management

Healthy soil is the foundation of a thriving crop, and proper soil preparation and management are essential for achieving successful cultivation. As farmers and gardeners, we know that our soil is a living, breathing ecosystem, and treating it with care and respect is key to bountiful harvests.

Conducting soil tests to assess nutrient levels, pH, and texture provides us with valuable insights for developing targeted soil amendments and fertilization strategies tailored to our crops' needs. By incorporating organic matter, such as compost or aged manure, we can improve soil structure, water-holding capacity, and nutrient availability, giving our plants the nourishment they need to thrive.

Implementing appropriate tillage methods, like no-till or minimum tillage, can also enhance soil health by reducing erosion, conserving moisture, and promoting beneficial soil biology. And let's not forget the power of cover cropping — planting cover crops during fallow periods can prevent soil erosion, suppress weeds, and replenish soil nutrients through nitrogen fixation or nutrient scavenging.

Crop Selection and Rotation

Selecting suitable crop varieties and implementing crop rotation strategies are crucial steps in optimizing yields, managing pests and diseases, and maintaining soil fertility. As stewards of the land, it's our responsibility to choose wisely and plan ahead.

When selecting crops, we must consider our local climate, temperature ranges, and precipitation patterns. Choosing crop varieties adapted to these conditions can improve crop performance and resilience, increasing our chances of success.

Different crops also have varying soil preferences, including nutrient needs, pH levels, and drainage requirements. By understanding these preferences and rotating crops from different plant families, we can disrupt pest and disease cycles, replenish soil nutrients, and improve soil structure — a win-win for our crops and our land.

Planting and Sowing

With careful preparation and the right crop selections, it's time to turn our attention to the planting and sowing process. Proper techniques in this stage can significantly impact crop establishment, growth, and yield potential, setting the stage for a bountiful harvest.

Sourcing high-quality, disease-free seeds or seedlings from reputable suppliers is essential for optimal germination and vigor. Like a strong foundation for a building, starting with robust and healthy plant material gives our crops the best chance to thrive.

Following recommended planting depths and spacing guidelines specific to each crop is also crucial. By providing our plants with the space and resources they need, we can optimize resource utilization and prevent overcrowding or competition, allowing each plant to reach its full potential.

Timing is everything, and planting at the appropriate time, considering factors like soil temperature, frost dates, and rainfall patterns, can improve crop establishment and growth. By working in harmony with nature's rhythms, we increase our chances of success.

Nutrient Management and Fertilization

Just as we need proper nourishment to thrive, our crops require adequate nutrients for optimal growth, yield, and quality. As responsible farmers and gardeners, we must ensure that our plants receive the nutrients they need while minimizing our environmental impact.

Incorporating organic fertilizers, such as compost, manure, or green manures, can provide a slow-release source of nutrients and improve soil health. These natural amendments not only feed our plants but also contribute to the overall well-being of the soil ecosystem.

In cases where nutrient deficiencies persist, judicious use of synthetic fertilizers, applied based on soil test recommendations and crop requirements, can supplement the nutrient needs of our plants. However, we must be mindful of the potential environmental impacts and strive for responsible and efficient application.

Foliar fertilizers, which are liquid fertilizers applied directly to the plant leaves, can provide a quick nutrient boost during critical growth stages, ensuring our crops have the necessary resources when they need them most.

Fertigation, the combination of fertilizer application with irrigation systems, is another efficient method of nutrient delivery and uptake by plants, minimizing waste and optimizing resource utilization.

Pest and Disease Control

Despite our best efforts, pests and diseases can sometimes threaten our crops. However, as responsible farmers and gardeners, we have a range of strategies at our disposal to manage these challenges effectively while minimizing environmental impacts.

Implementing Integrated Pest Management (IPM) strategies, which combine multiple control methods, including cultural, biological, and judicious chemical control, can help us manage pests and diseases effectively. By understanding the life cycles and behaviors of these threats, we can develop targeted and sustainable solutions.

Introducing natural enemies, such as beneficial insects or microorganisms, can help control pests and diseases through natural predation or competition, fostering a balanced ecosystem within our fields and gardens.

Cultural control practices, like crop rotation, sanitation, and the use of resistant varieties, can disrupt pest and disease cycles and reduce their incidence, empowering us to work in harmony with nature's defenses.

When necessary, applying targeted and approved pesticides according to label instructions and integrated pest management principles can effectively control pests and diseases while minimizing risks to human health and the environment.

Harvesting and Post-Harvest Handling

After months of hard work and dedication, the moment we've all been waiting for — harvest time! But our efforts don't stop there. Proper harvesting techniques and post-harvest handling practices are crucial for preserving crop quality, extending shelf life, and minimizing losses, ensuring that our labors bear the sweetest fruits.

Timely harvesting, when crops have reached their optimal maturity stage, ensures maximum quality, flavor, and nutritional value, rewarding us for our patience and commitment.

Using appropriate tools and containers during harvesting and transportation can prevent physical damage and contamination, preserving the integrity of our hard-earned produce.

Certain crops, like onions or grains, may require curing or drying processes to enhance storage life and quality, allowing us to enjoy the fruits of our labor for an extended period.

Maintaining appropriate temperature, humidity, and ventilation during storage can prevent spoilage, insect infestations, and quality deterioration, ensuring that our efforts don't go to waste.

For those looking to add value to their crops, techniques like canning, freezing, or processing into value-added products can extend shelf life and increase profitability, opening up new opportunities for our farming endeavors.

By implementing these farming practices and techniques, we, as small-scale farmers and home gardeners, can optimize crop yields, maintain soil health, manage pests and diseases effectively, and ensure high-quality produce while promoting sustainable and environmentally responsible agriculture practices that respect and nurture our land.

Agricultural Technology and Software

In today's rapidly evolving agricultural landscape, technology and software are playing an increasingly vital role in supporting our successful crop cultivation efforts as small-scale farmers and home gardeners. From farm management tools to cutting-edge precision agriculture technologies, these advancements offer valuable resources for optimizing our operations, increasing efficiency, and promoting sustainable practices.

Useful Apps and Software for Farmers

The proliferation of mobile devices and user-friendly software has made it easier than ever for us farmers and gardeners to access valuable information and tools right at our fingertips. No more scouring through dusty old tomes or relying solely on word-of-mouth — the digital age has brought a wealth of knowledge and resources to our doorsteps.

Farm Management Software

Farm management software solutions are designed to streamline various aspects of our farm operations, including crop planning, record-keeping, inventory management, and financial tracking. These tools can help us stay organized, make informed decisions, and ensure efficient resource allocation, taking some of the guesswork out of our daily tasks.

Solutions like FarmLogs, a cloud-based platform, allow us to track field activities, manage inputs (seeds, fertilizers, pesticides), and analyze yield data for better decision-making. Granular offers a suite of tools for crop planning, input tracking, and yield analysis, helping us optimize our operations and maximize profitability. For those of us running small-scale or urban farms, FarmQA provides record-keeping, task management, and inventory tracking features tailored to our unique needs.

Weather and Climate Monitoring Apps

Accurate weather and climate information is crucial for making informed decisions about planting, irrigation, and pest management. That's where mobile apps like WeatherBug, Dark Sky, and RainedOut come in handy, offering real-time weather data, forecasts, and customizable alerts to help us stay ahead of changing conditions. With these tools at our fingertips, we can better prepare for potential challenges and make proactive decisions to protect our crops.

Crop Monitoring and Precision Agriculture Tools

Precision agriculture tools leverage advanced technologies to monitor crop health, identify issues, and optimize input applications. These tools can be particularly valuable for us small-scale farmers and home gardeners seeking to maximize yields while minimizing resource use and our environmental impact.

Imagine being able to identify plant diseases, pests, and nutrient deficiencies just by snapping a picture with your smartphone! Apps like Plantix and Agrobase use image recognition and machine learning to do just that, providing us with recommendations for targeted interventions to keep our crops thriving.

And what about soil sensors like those from Edyn or CropX? These nifty devices measure soil moisture, temperature, and nutrient levels, allowing us to optimize irrigation and fertilization practices, ensuring our plants get the perfect amount of water and nutrients they need when they need it.

For those of us with a bird's eye view, unmanned aerial vehicles (UAVs) equipped with cameras or multispectral sensors can capture high-resolution imagery of our crop fields, enabling early detection of stress or problem areas. This cutting-edge technology empowers us to take proactive measures and address issues before they become major setbacks.

Emerging Technologies in Agriculture

But that's just the tip of the iceberg! Several cutting-edge technologies are reshaping the agricultural landscape, offering exciting possibilities for us small-scale farmers and home gardeners to embrace sustainable and efficient practices.

Precision Agriculture and Sensor Technologies

Precision agriculture involves the use of advanced sensors, GPS, and data analysis to optimize input application and crop management practices. These technologies can help us maximize yields while minimizing waste and environmental impact, striking that delicate balance we all strive for.

Variable Rate Technology (VRT), for instance, combines GPS data with soil and crop data to allow us to apply inputs (fertilizers, pesticides) at variable rates based on specific field conditions. No more blanket applications and potential over-application — with VRT, we can be precise and efficient, reducing waste and saving resources.

And let's not forget about remote sensing! Satellite or aerial imagery combined with advanced data analytics can provide detailed information on crop health, yield potential, and nutrient status, enabling us to make timely interventions and develop targeted management strategies. It's like having a team of highly trained scouts keeping a watchful eye on our fields and gardens.

Automation and Robotics

Automation and robotics are revolutionizing agricultural operations, offering solutions for labor-intensive tasks and enhancing efficiency. While large-scale adoption may be more feasible for commercial operations, some applications can benefit us, small-scale farmers and home gardeners, too.

Imagine having an automated irrigation system that uses sensors and controllers to deliver precise amounts of water based on real-time soil moisture data. No more guesswork or water waste — just efficient, targeted irrigation that keeps our plants happy and our water bills low.

Then there are the robotic weeders and harvesters. These automated robots can perform tasks like weeding, thinning, and harvesting, reducing our labor requirements and minimizing crop damage. It's like having an extra set of hands (or wheels!) in the field or garden, freeing us up to focus on other tasks or simply take a well-deserved break.

Biotechnology and Genetic Engineering

Advances in biotechnology and genetic engineering also offer potential solutions for improving crop yields, enhancing resilience, and addressing global challenges like climate change and food security – issues that impact us all, no matter the scale of our operations.

While genetically modified (GM) crops remain a topic of discussion and debate, engineered traits like pest resistance, drought tolerance, or improved nutritional content could benefit us small-scale farmers and home gardeners in challenging environments, helping us overcome obstacles and produce more with less.

Gene editing techniques like CRISPR-Cas9 allow for targeted modifications in crop genomes, enabling the development of new varieties with desirable traits without introducing foreign genes. It's like giving nature a helping hand, but with a delicate touch.

Beneficial microorganisms, like plant growth-promoting bacteria or fungi, can also be applied as inoculants to improve nutrient uptake, stress tolerance, and overall plant health. Think of them as tiny helpers, working tirelessly in the soil to give our crops a boost.

While some of these emerging technologies may be more accessible to larger commercial operations for now, their potential to improve efficiency, sustainability, and resilience could trickle down to us small-scale farmers and home gardeners as costs decrease and adoption rates increase.

It's important for us to approach the adoption of agricultural technologies and software thoughtfully, considering factors like cost-effectiveness, ease of use, and compatibility with our existing practices. Additionally, proper training and education are essential to ensure effective implementation and maximize the benefits of these tools.

By embracing appropriate technologies and software solutions, we can enhance our crop cultivation practices, optimize resource use, and stay competitive in an increasingly technology-driven agricultural landscape, all while staying true to our values of sustainability and environmental stewardship.

Networking and Community Engagement in Agriculture

While advanced technologies and farming practices are crucial for our successful crop cultivation, networking and community engagement play an equally important role in supporting us, small-scale farmers and home gardeners. Building connections within the agricultural community fosters knowledge sharing, promotes sustainable practices, and creates support systems that contribute to the overall success and resilience of our local food systems.

The Role of Agricultural Networks

Agricultural networks serve as vital platforms for us farmers and gardeners to connect, collaborate, and access valuable resources. These networks can take various forms, including local organizations, regional cooperatives, or national associations. And their primary roles are invaluable.

First and foremost, networks facilitate the exchange of information, best practices, and innovative techniques among members, promoting continuous learning and adaptation. We can share our successes, learn from our failures, and collectively push the boundaries of what's possible in sustainable agriculture.

Additionally, networks often provide access to shared resources, such as equipment, marketing channels, or bulk purchasing opportunities. For those of us running small-scale operations with limited resources, these shared assets can be game-changers, allowing us to leverage economies of scale and access tools and markets that might otherwise be out of reach.

But perhaps most importantly, by uniting our voices, agricultural networks can effectively advocate for policies and regulations that support sustainable farming practices and protect the interests of small-scale producers like us. Together, we can create a powerful force for positive change in the agricultural landscape.

Farmer-to-Farmer Networks and Knowledge Sharing

One of the most valuable aspects of agricultural networks is the opportunity for farmer-to-farmer knowledge sharing. These peer-to-peer exchanges allow experienced farmers and gardeners to share their hard-earned expertise, lessons learned, and practical solutions with others facing similar challenges. It's like having a collective brain trust at our fingertips.

Community Supported Agriculture (CSA) groups are a prime example of this. As members of a CSA, we often form tight-knit communities where knowledge and experiences are shared through regular interactions and farm visits. We learn from each other, support each other, and grow together, both literally and figuratively.

Farmer Field Schools are another excellent example of farmer-to-farmer networks. These informal groups facilitate hands-on learning and experience sharing among farmers, focusing on topics like integrated pest management, soil health, or crop-specific techniques. By pooling our collective knowledge, we can overcome challenges more effectively and develop sustainable solutions that work for our local conditions.

Regional Grower Associations also play a vital role, bringing together farmers and gardeners within a specific geographic area. These associations foster networking, knowledge exchange, and collaborative problem-solving, creating a sense of community and shared purpose among those of us working the land.

Community Engagement and Local Support Systems

Successful crop cultivation extends beyond the farm gate and relies on the support and engagement of our local communities. Strong community ties and support systems can provide numerous benefits for us small-scale farmers and home gardeners.

Direct sales of our produce through farmers' markets, farm stands, or community-supported agriculture (CSA) programs not only provide a reliable source of income but also promote and strengthen our local food systems. By engaging with our communities, we create a direct connection between the people and their food, fostering a deeper appreciation for the hard work and care that goes into every harvest.

Community members can also contribute valuable labor and volunteer assistance during peak seasons or for specific farming tasks, alleviating the burden on our small-scale operations. It's a beautiful symbiosis — we provide nourishment for our communities, and they, in turn, lend a helping hand when we need it most.

Engaging with local schools, community gardens, or educational initiatives can also create opportunities for knowledge sharing, skills development, and promoting the values of sustainable agriculture to future generations. By inspiring and empowering the next generation of farmers and gardeners, we can ensure that our hard work and philosophies live on, creating a more sustainable and resilient food system for years to come.

The Impact of Social Media and Online Communities

In the digital age, social media and online communities have emerged as powerful platforms for networking and knowledge sharing within the agricultural sector. These virtual spaces offer numerous benefits for us small-scale farmers and home gardeners, breaking down geographical barriers and connecting us with like-minded individuals from around the globe.

Online forums, social media groups, and platforms like YouTube allow us to share tips, seek advice, and troubleshoot problems in real-time, fostering a collaborative learning environment that transcends physical boundaries. We can learn from farmers and gardeners in different regions, climates, and cultures, expanding our horizons and broadening our understanding of sustainable practices.

Social media channels and e-commerce platforms also provide new avenues for marketing and selling our produce, expanding the reach of our small-scale operations beyond our local communities. With a few clicks, we can connect with customers near and far, sharing the fruits of our labor with a wider audience.

And let's not forget the power of online communities for raising awareness about sustainable agriculture practices, promoting local food systems, and advocating for policies that support small-scale farmers and home gardeners like us. By harnessing the collective voice of our virtual communities, we can create a ripple effect that resonates far beyond our individual spheres of influence.

However, as we navigate these online spaces, it's essential to approach them with a critical eye, verifying information from reliable sources and exercising caution regarding potential misinformation or unsuitable recommendations. By fostering a spirit of healthy skepticism and diligent fact-checking, we can ensure that our online communities remain bastions of trustworthy knowledge and support.

By actively engaging in agricultural networks, fostering community connections, and leveraging the power of social media and online communities, we small-scale farmers and home gardeners can access invaluable resources, support systems, and opportunities for growth and success in our crop cultivation endeavors. Together, we can build a more sustainable, resilient, and equitable food system, one harvest at a time.

Conclusion and Future Prospects

As we've explored throughout this chapter, successful crop cultivation for small-scale farmers and home gardeners like ourselves is a multifaceted endeavor that requires a combination of essential resources, practical farming techniques, appropriate technology adoption, and strong community engagement. We've delved into the importance of accessing reliable information sources, utilizing efficient tools and equipment, implementing sustainable farming practices, and leveraging emerging agricultural technologies.

Moreover, we've highlighted the vital role of networking and community involvement in fostering knowledge sharing, providing support systems, and promoting resilient local food systems. By embracing these key elements, we can optimize our crop yields, enhance resource efficiency, and contribute to environmental sustainability while maintaining economic viability — a true win-win for our farms, our communities, and our planet.

Challenges and Opportunities in Sustainable Agriculture

While the pursuit of successful crop cultivation presents its fair share of challenges, it also offers promising opportunities for us small-scale farmers and home gardeners to contribute to sustainable agriculture and food security. Let's take a closer look at some of the key challenges and opportunities:

Challenges

Climate Change Impacts: Unpredictable weather patterns, extreme weather events, and shifting growing seasons pose significant challenges for our crop cultivation efforts, requiring us to adapt and develop resilience strategies.

Access to Resources and Technology: Limited access to resources, including land, water, and financial capital, as well as the affordability of emerging technologies, can hinder our ability to adopt sustainable practices and efficiency-enhancing tools.

Market Access and Fair Pricing: As small-scale farmers, we often face challenges in accessing profitable markets and receiving fair prices for our produce, which can undermine our economic sustainability.

Opportunities:

Growing Demand for Local and Sustainable Food: Increasing consumer awareness and demand for locally grown, sustainable, and organic produce create exciting market opportunities for us small-scale farmers and home gardeners to tap into.

Regenerative Agriculture and Soil Health: Practices that promote soil health, such as cover cropping, no-till farming, and organic amendments, can enhance long-term productivity and environmental sustainability, ensuring that our land remains fertile and productive for generations to come.

Urban Agriculture and Community Gardens: The rise of urban agriculture and community gardens presents opportunities for city dwellers to engage in small-scale food production, promoting food security and community resilience and bringing the joys and benefits of farming closer to home.

Future Trends and Developments

The agricultural landscape is continuously evolving, driven by technological advancements, changing consumer preferences, and the need for sustainable solutions. Here are some future trends and developments that may shape successful crop cultivation for small-scale farmers and home gardeners:

Precision Agriculture and Smart Farming: The integration of sensors, drones, robotics, and advanced data analytics will enable more precise and efficient crop management, optimizing inputs and minimizing waste, making sustainable practices more accessible and effective.

Vertical and Controlled Environment Agriculture: Controlled environment agriculture systems, such as vertical farming and greenhouse operations, may become more accessible and affordable, allowing us to produce year-round and utilize resources more efficiently.

Agroecological Approaches: Increasing emphasis on agroecological principles, such as biodiversity conservation, ecosystem services, and traditional ecological knowledge, may promote more sustainable and resilient farming systems that work in harmony with nature rather than against it.

Biotechnology and Gene Editing: Continued advancements in biotechnology and gene editing techniques may lead to the development of crop varieties with enhanced traits, such as improved nutrition, disease resistance, and climate resilience. While this remains a topic of debate, these advancements could potentially benefit us by helping overcome agricultural challenges.

Circular and Regenerative Systems: The adoption of circular and regenerative agricultural systems, which aim to minimize waste and promote closed-loop nutrient cycles, may gain traction as a sustainable approach to crop cultivation. By mimicking nature's processes, we can create a more efficient and environmentally friendly way of farming.

As the agricultural landscape evolves, we small-scale farmers and home gardeners must remain adaptable, open to innovation, and committed to sustainable practices. By embracing emerging trends and technologies while preserving traditional knowledge, we can contribute to a more resilient and sustainable food system for generations to come.

And let's not forget the importance of maintaining a sense of wonder and connection to the land we cultivate. While advancements in technology and science are invaluable tools, we must never lose sight of the profound beauty and magic that lies in the simple act of tending to our crops, nurturing them from seed to harvest.

The feeling of sun-warmed soil between our fingers, the gentle rustle of leaves in the breeze, the vibrant colors of ripe produce — these are the moments that remind us why we do what we do. It's not just about feeding ourselves and our communities; it's about reconnecting with the rhythms of nature, the cycles of life that have sustained humanity since the dawn of agriculture.

So, let us move forward with open minds and open hearts, embracing the tools and knowledge that can help us become better stewards of the land while never losing sight of the profound beauty and spirituality that lies at the heart of our craft.

We are not just farmers and gardeners; we are caretakers, nurturers, and custodians of a sacred tradition that has sustained civilizations for millennia. And it is with this reverence and respect for the land that we will build a more sustainable, equitable, and nourishing future for all.

Chapter Ten — A Substantial Path Forward

As we approach the conclusion of this journey through the principles and practices of regenerative agriculture, it's essential to pause and reflect on the ground we've covered and the insights gained along the way. For those of you tending to small farms or backyard gardens, I hope this book has provided a comprehensive roadmap for nurturing healthy soils, bountiful harvests, and a more sustainable approach to cultivating the land.

We began by delving into the foundational concepts of regenerative agriculture, recognizing the pivotal role that soil health plays in ensuring the vitality and resilience of our crops. By understanding the intricate web of life teeming beneath our feet, we've learned to treat our soils not merely as an inert growing medium but as a living, breathing ecosystem deserving of our utmost care and respect.

From there, we embarked on a holistic exploration of strategies to build and maintain fertile soils. We discussed the merits of cover cropping, composting, and natural fertilizers, each offering a means to replenish the nutrients and organic matter that are the lifeblood of thriving plant life. We also examined the virtues of crop rotation, diversified planting, and companion planting, techniques that mimic nature's inherent biodiversity and foster a balanced, self-sustaining agricultural system.

Water, that indispensable elixir of life, received its due attention as we delved into efficient irrigation practices, rainwater harvesting, and soil moisture monitoring. By optimizing our use of this precious resource, we can ensure the vitality of our crops while minimizing our environmental footprint.

Furthermore, we explored the transformative potential of regenerative practices such as no-till farming, agroforestry, and natural pest management. These methods not only enhance soil health and crop productivity but also contribute to the broader goal of ecosystem restoration and environmental stewardship.

Throughout our journey, we've encountered inspiring case studies and real-world examples that illustrate the tangible benefits of adopting regenerative approaches. From small-scale family farms to large-scale commercial operations, the success stories showcased the resilience, innovation, and adaptability of those who have embraced a more sustainable path.

Practical Strategies and Tips for Implementing Regenerative Agriculture

While the principles and theories of regenerative agriculture are invaluable, their true power lies in their practical application on the land. As you embark on your own regenerative journey, consider implementing the following strategies and tips:

1. **Start small and manageable:** Transitioning to regenerative practices can seem daunting, especially if you're accustomed to conventional methods. Begin by designating a small portion of your land or garden as a testing ground, where you can experiment with cover crops, composting, or no-till techniques without overhauling your entire operation. As you gain experience and confidence, gradually expand these practices to larger areas.
2. **Observe and adapt:** Regenerative agriculture is not a one-size-fits-all approach; it requires an intimate understanding of your unique environment, climate, and soil conditions. Become an avid observer of your land, taking note of how different practices influence soil structure, water retention, and plant health. Don't be afraid to adjust and refine your methods based on your observations and experiences.
3. **Embrace diversity:** One of the core tenets of regenerative agriculture is the promotion of biodiversity. Incorporate a diverse array of crops, cover crops, and companion plants into your rotations. Encourage beneficial insects and pollinators

by planting flowering plants and creating habitats. This diversity will not only enhance soil fertility and pest resistance but also provide a more resilient and vibrant ecosystem.

Tip: When selecting cover crops, consider mixing multiple species together, such as legumes, grasses, and brassicas. This diverse "cocktail" of cover crops can provide a wider range of benefits and better mimic the complexity of natural ecosystems.

4. **Engage in community learning:** Seek out local farmer networks, community gardens, or extension services where you can learn from experienced practitioners and share your own experiences. Attend workshops, field days, or conferences focused on regenerative agriculture to expand your knowledge and connect with like-minded individuals. The collective wisdom of these communities can be invaluable in overcoming challenges and refining your practices.

Trick: Don't be afraid to ask questions, even seemingly basic ones. Seasoned regenerative farmers are often eager to share their hard-earned knowledge and may offer insights or solutions you hadn't considered.

5. **Monitor and record:** Regularly assess the health of your soils, crops, and overall ecosystem through various monitoring techniques, such as soil testing, yield tracking, and biodiversity assessments. Keep detailed records of your practices, observations, and outcomes, as this data can guide future decisions and help you identify areas for improvement.

Tip: Consider setting up a simple field notebook or digital journal to document your regenerative practices, noting details such as planting dates, crop rotations, soil amendments, and any notable observations or challenges faced.

6. **Be patient and persistent:** Transitioning to regenerative agriculture is a journey, not a destination. It may take several growing seasons to fully realize the benefits of your efforts as soil health and ecosystem balance are gradually restored. Remain patient, persistent, and committed to your long-term vision of a sustainable and thriving agricultural system.

   Trick: Celebrate small victories along the way, such as improved soil structure, increased biodiversity, or a bountiful harvest of a particular crop. These milestones will fuel your motivation and remind you of the progress you're making.

7. **Experiment with natural remedies:** In addition to implementing regenerative practices, explore the use of natural remedies and inputs to address common agricultural challenges. For example, certain plant extracts or essential oils can act as effective insect repellents or fungicides, while beneficial microorganisms can enhance soil fertility and plant growth.

   Tip: Research traditional and indigenous agricultural practices from your region or similar climates. These time-honored methods often rely on locally available natural resources and can offer valuable insights into sustainable farming techniques.

8. **Embrace permaculture principles:** Permaculture, a design philosophy that emphasizes the harmonious integration of human settlements with natural systems, can complement and enhance regenerative agriculture practices. Principles such as zoning, efficient energy planning, and utilizing renewable resources can help you create a more self-sufficient and sustainable growing environment.

    Trick: When designing your regenerative growing space, consider integrating elements such as swales (shallow trenches) for water harvesting, hugelkultur mounds (raised beds with buried wood) for moisture retention, and strategically placed windbreaks or shade structures.

9. **Foster a connection with the land:** Regenerative agriculture is not just a set of practices; it's a mindset and a way of life that recognizes our profound connection to the natural world. Spend time in your fields or garden, observing the intricate relationships between plants, animals, and the soil. Allow this connection to deepen your appreciation for the land and guide your decision-making.

    Tip: Consider incorporating mindfulness practices, such as meditation or nature journaling, into your agricultural routine. These activities can heighten your awareness and attunement to the rhythms and cycles of the land.

Ultimately, regenerative agriculture is about more than just crop yields and profits; it's about cultivating a harmonious relationship with the land, respecting the delicate balance of nature, and ensuring that we leave behind a legacy of abundance and stewardship for future generations.

As you embark on this transformative path, remember that the journey is as important as the destination. Embrace the lessons nature has to offer, and allow your connection to the land to deepen with each passing season. Through patience, perseverance, and a willingness to learn and adapt, you will not only nurture your crops but also contribute to a more regenerative and sustainable future for our planet.

Milton Keynes UK
Ingram Content Group UK Ltd.
UKHW032050231124
451423UK00013B/1161